VALHALLA'S
WAKE

ALSO BY JOHN LOFTUS

The Belarus Secret

VALHALLA'S
W A K E

The IRA, MI6, and
the Assassination of
a Young American

JOHN LOFTUS and
EMILY McINTYRE

THE ATLANTIC MONTHLY PRESS
NEW YORK

To my son, John,

who loved the children of Ireland and could not be indifferent
to their pain. Whatever he may have done, he did not deserve
to die.

Emily McIntyre

Published simultaneously in Canada
Printed in the United States of America
FIRST EDITION

Library of Congress Cataloging-in-Publication Data
Loftus, John.
Valhalla's wake : the IRA, MI6, and the assassination
of a young American / John Loftus & Emily McIntyre.—1st ed.
ISBN 0-87113-247-8
1. Northern Ireland—Politics and government—1969– 2. McIntyre,
John, 1952–1984. 3. Irish Republican Army. 4. Smuggling—Northern
Ireland. 5. Smuggling—Massachusetts. 6. Munitions—Northern
Ireland. 7. Munitions—Massachusetts. I. McIntyre, Emily.
II. Title.
DA990.U46L66 1989 89-32163 941.60824—dc20

The Atlantic Monthly Press
19 Union Square West
New York, NY 10003

FIRST PRINTING

ACKNOWLEDGMENTS

Special thanks are due to those brave men and women of the Israeli, Irish, British, West German, and American intelligence services who came forward to assist Emily and me. Although *Valhalla's Wake* was submitted to the U.S. government for a national security review, they are not responsible for its contents. For reasons of privacy, the name "Chuck" is used as a composite of John's male friends, and "Robbi" is used for females.

I am especially indebted to Chris, the last of the McIntyres, for his tireless work, and to the many members of the bar and press who patiently suggested corrections for the manuscript. After many drafts, this is as close as anyone may ever come to the complete truth until the British Intelligence files are declassified. The errors that remain are mine alone.

Finally, and most importantly, I must thank my wife, Susan, without whose love and support I could never have finished this book. Susan, a child of England, allowed me, a child of Ireland, to keep a promise I made to a dying friend, John McIntyre, Sr. I hope that I have told his story well.

JOHN LOFTUS
Saint Petersburg, Florida

CONTENTS

1

FIASCO AT SEA

Generations of American fishermen have sailed from Gloucester Harbor to the fertile fishing grounds off the North Atlantic
coast. A statue of a young mariner, buffeted by rain and wind,
tarnished hands wedded to his ship's wheel, stares out to sea
from the promenade along the Gloucester shoreline. He
stands as an enduring testament to Gloucester's finest and to
the risks they took on often-hostile seas, "They that go down
to the sea in ships."

Captain Bob Anderson, a powerfully built six-footer of
Norwegian ancestry, was an orphan of this proud tradition.
His heritage ran in a direct line from the buccaneers of old to
the rumrunners of a less-distant past. Anderson was a modern-day maritime soldier of fortune, ferrying whatever would
bring the best price.

Anderson's reasoning was simple. For the hard-working
Italian, Irish, and Portuguese fishermen whose trawlers filled
Gloucester Harbor, a good catch of lobster or haddock, or even
the swordfish Anderson fished illegally, might net a living
wage. But upkeep and labor costs had to be factored in, to say
nothing of the days and nights spent fighting the notoriously
terrible weather off Georges Bank.

Drugs, on the other hand—marijuana, hashish, and for

the last few years, cocaine—with their potential for grand and quick profit, seduced fishermen by the score along the bays and inlets that peppered the New England coast.

Anderson had been won over by the promise of easy money for little risk. A single run to the Corsair Canyon in the Gulf of Maine, where he could pick up a cargo of hashish from a mother ship and then ferry it to another vessel in Long Island Sound, destined for the insatiable New York market, might net him a fast, tax-free $150,000. True, he had on one occasion lost the roll of the dice and been caught smuggling illegal swordfish. His boat, the *Kristen Lee*, a steel-hulled seventy-five foot trawler of the kind most favored by New England smugglers, had been seized by the Coast Guard. But like bankruptcy to a commodities trader, Anderson blithely counted such travails as one of the costs of working at his trade.

Until his operation was busted wide open in the early eighties, Frankie LePere owned the Mafia's drug franchise from Boston south to Cape Cod. Counterfeiting, cocaine, and marijuana were the staples of his trade. LePere had begun business in Plymouth, the home of the *Mayflower*, hiding cocaine in lobster pots offshore. Fishermen would later haul the pots in, pluck out the coke, and throw the errant lobsters back into the sea.

Anderson was hired by LePere when he expanded his drug-running organization. Anderson worked as a skipper on runs from Corsair Canyon and waited for an opportunity to reclaim the *Kristen Lee* from her new owners—the U.S. government.

Anderson's connection to Frankie LePere won him the trust of Joe Murray, LePere's successor in the drug-importing business. For years, this Boston Irishman had dabbled in marijuana, but in 1983 secretly expanded into narcotics, counterfeiting, and fencing operations for the Mafia. His territory ranged from Winter Hill, in the Boston suburb of Revere, north to the industrial city of Lynn and the tony bedroom communities of the North Shore.

Murray stood just over six feet and weighed 230 pounds. His large, square head and lineman's bullish neck were mellowed by the designer wire-rimmed glasses he wore, but he still cut an intimidating figure. Joe's closely cropped hair, so fair it was nearly white, receded from his temples and made him look older than his forty-odd years.

Murray didn't trust many people. Few, apart from Anderson, knew of his role as Mafia kingpin. He was secretive and closemouthed. He would only drink in the comfort and privacy of his own home, where he couldn't be hurt by the names, places, and payoffs slipping from his liquor-loosened tongue.

Joe wasn't a friendly, back-slapping guy, but then Charlestown wasn't always congenial to the Italian Mafia. And Joe, though Irish, was becoming the underworld mayor of Charlestown. He was most at ease in a T-shirt and jeans, with a glass of water in his hand (even though his income would suggest a Perrier): the Mob viewed him as their answer to Don Corleone in the toughest section of Boston. The Irish "townies," however, had a different perspective.

Murray was the only person the poor Charlestown Irish could turn to when the Boston Redevelopment Authority announced plans to take their houses by eminent domain or when mothers were worried about young toughs courting their daughters. Joe never promised to solve their problems, but he always ended up doing so. And when he asked a favor in return, it was always granted, no questions asked. Such was life in the shadow of Bunker Hill, where generations of Irish-Americans who had grown up in squat projects were moving into triple deckers with no further aspirations beyond getting through the day. Here, Joe Murray was king. None of his neighbors realized this local pub owner had amassed a fortune working for the Mob.

VALHALLA'S WAKE

When Bob Anderson arrived at Murray's unassuming two-family home in Charlestown on July 12, 1984, he had every reason to suppose Joe was preparing another offshore transfer of drugs and needed the services of a reliable captain. He was half wrong.

Murray worked for the Mob, but he was an Irishman just the same and a willing soldier in the Provisional wing of the IRA. For a long time, the IRA had been satisfied with the occasional contributions Murray skimmed off his bar profits and his willingness to use his connections in Charlestown to provide for fugitives who made their way to Boston along the IRA's version of the Underground Railway.

During 1984, the IRA planned a major change in its strategy of armed confrontation with the British army in Northern Ireland. The bombing of the seaside hotel in Brighton where British Prime Minister Margaret Thatcher and most of her Tory cabinet were staying during the annual Conservative party conference in the fall of 1984 was a sharp signal of this new program. A series of quick military assaults on British bases and police stations in Northern Ireland was planned to complement the political assassinations, together creating irresistible pressure for British withdrawal.

To bring the war directly to the British, the weapons-starved Provos required enough matériel to outfit a company of soldiers. Murray had been ordered to assemble this arsenal and to run the largest IRA shipment of guns in a decade out of Boston. Ever the cautious businessman, he wasn't enthusiastic about this new venture. Sean Crawley, an IRA operative and former member of the elite U.S. Navy SEAL commandos who had lived in Ireland since 1979, was sent to Boston to coordinate the procurement of arms.

Murray needed a skipper he could depend on to ferry the guns to an IRA ship near Porcupine Bank, one hundred miles off the Irish coast. Murray asked Bob Anderson if he would transport the guns for a six-figure fee. Anderson had long ago

4

stopped caring what cargo he was hauling. As long as the price was right, he said, he would.

On September 11, and then again on the twelfth, the *Valhalla*, a nondescript, beamy fishing trawler complete with girder-like outriggers pointing skyward on both port and starboard, picked up twenty-six tons of crushed ice and 7,899 gallons of fuel at Gloucester Marine Railways in preparation for some offshore swordfishing—at least, that was the cover story Anderson was using along the Gloucester waterfront. Except for the tangle of sophisticated electronics recently put in place over the newly painted pilothouse, the *Valhalla* might easily have been preparing for an extended run from Georges Bank to the Grand Banks, a rich fishing ground east of Newfoundland. On the night of the thirteenth, the *Valhalla* was loaded with the guns and sophisticated electronics that Murray had assembled at the dock of Anderson's A and M Trading Company.

The *Valhalla* headed out of port at one in the morning on September 14 with a shorthanded crew: Anderson, the captain; John McIntyre, a communications specialist acting as engineer and navigator; and Sean Crawley, who would leave the *Valhalla* and escort its cargo of weapons ashore.

No one in the world was happier than John McIntyre that night. Passionately committed to the IRA, John didn't realize the extent of Murray's conflicting loyalty to the Mafia. John had good reason to believe that if he hadn't pushed Murray to organize this arms transfer, Joe would still be putting all his energy into smuggling pot instead of running guns for the IRA.

Joe was John's IRA patron as well as mentor and friend. He had introduced John to the IRA eighteen months earlier, and John had assimilated its militant views with the revolutionary fervor of a twenty-nine-year-old. The British occupation of Ireland had to be ended, he believed, and the Provos were the only ones willing and able to do it. John was fond of borrowing one of his father's favorite quotes from Saint Thomas Aquinas to explain his conversion to superpatriot. As a last resort, Aquinas had written, violence may be used to overcome an unjust ruler.

Whenever John McIntyre had become committed to something larger than himself—the U.S. Army, or his on-again, off-again marriage—he had been sorely disappointed. John was a rebel looking for a crusade to focus his heartfelt enthusiasm for the underdog. More than anything, he wanted to belong to a noble cause worth fighting and dying for. John was certain that with the IRA, at long last, he had found his niche in life. He was born to be a freedom fighter. Now he was getting his chance and daring disappointment once again.

The day of the *Valhalla's* departure, John packed a three-volume history of Ireland and a 9mm handgun in his sea bag and kissed his girlfriend, Robbi, goodbye. Without telling anyone, he had taken his father's favorite blue baseball cap, with the words "Military Intelligence" embroidered on the front. John packed it in his sea bag for luck. Here he was, an undercover soldier in the IRA, going off to do secret battle.

Rigged with side-dragging nets hung off both port and starboard crane booms, the *Valhalla* did not attract any undue attention as it headed out of Gloucester Harbor, past the U.S. Coast Guard station, and out into open ocean east of Cape Ann. Nothing had been done to the *Valhalla* to differentiate it, at least outwardly, from the scores of boats that made many thousands of such departures every year from the small coastal town. The *Valhalla* was a freshly painted white above the waterline. Its hold had been loaded to capacity with ice; fuel filled the extra tanks John had welded for the long sea journey that stretched before them.

For Anderson, piloting the *Valhalla* was like taking up with an old lover. After his seventy-five-foot fishing trawler

Fiasco at Sea

was seized by U.S. Customs agents in January 1981 for illegal swordfishing, it sat rotting at the customs dock until Anderson, by then working for Joe Murray, bought it from the U.S. Marshals Service at government auction in July 1984. A newly incorporated company, Leeward Inc., fronting for McIntyre, paid almost a quarter of a million dollars for the vessel.

To Anderson, the price was well worth paying. Like all drug runners, he made every effort to buy his boat back from the government. Each trawler is an individual with a personality all its own. Anderson knew what the *Valhalla* was capable of and what to look for when something went wrong. This intimate familiarity could easily provide the margin of safety necessary for a North Atlantic crossing in hurricane season.

However comfortable Anderson was with the *Valhalla*, luck had not been running with IRA gun smugglers. No matter whether the gun smuggling originated in the Middle East or Europe, every shipment to the Provos since the early seventies had been intercepted and its contents seized.

The first seizure occurred on March 28, 1973. Five tons of Libyan mines, guns, and ammunition aboard the Cyprus-based *Claudia* were seized by the Irish Navy, prompting Britain to suspend arms deliveries to Colonel Muammar al-Qadhafi one month later. Six other attempts followed during the next ten years, all equally disastrous. There was no secret to these failures—except to the IRA. Its gun-running operation had been penetrated by a mole working for the British Secret Intelligence Service. Electronic bugs planted on each vessel had compromised each smuggling effort in succession.

McIntyre, a crackerjack former U.S. Army expert in electronic intelligence, was determined to end the IRA's legacy of incompetence and failure. He went to great lengths to assure security for this voyage. Before leaving Gloucester, John swept the *Valhalla* and its cargo for electronic homing devices.

Aside from the top Provo leadership in Ireland, only four

people in the U.S. knew the secret details of the weapons transfer. Two of them, John McIntyre and Sean Crawley, would be on the *Valhalla*. Joe Murray and Pat Nee—a Mafia confederate who was to South Boston what Murray was to Charlestown—would fly to Ireland, where Nee would then wait onshore with a hired truck. Murray would sail out to meet the *Valhalla* aboard the IRA rendezvous ship, a decrepit, wooden fishing trawler named the *Marita Ann*.

He was supposed to keep both captain and crew aboard the *Marita Ann* ignorant of their destination and their true mission until they were on their way to the rendezvous where they would offload Sean and the guns. John McIntyre had insisted that only he and Murray know the mid-ocean coordinates where the *Valhalla* was to meet the red and white *Marita Ann*, which would bear the weapons safely to Ireland. Once the boat docked, Pat Nee would drive Sean to a safe hiding place, known only to Pat. John had made sure that the IRA had restricted knowledge of the plan to those in the highest councils with a need to know. He was determined that the transfer would not be compromised by a leak to the U.S. Drug Enforcement Administration (DEA) and customs, who had already tried and failed to convict Murray for drug offenses, or to the British, who had their own retinue of spies hovering around Boston's docks and Irish bars. John had made Murray promise to stop his marijuana smuggling until the guns were safely ashore in Ireland.

There was no denying that John was attracted to the stealth and secrecy of his illegal enterprise, but he had too much of a sense of humor to see himself as a real-life version of the macho gung-ho adventures popularized in the copies of *Soldier of Fortune* that Sean had brought along for the journey. Before John left Boston, his girlfriend Robbi had given him a framed "Hagar the Horrible" cartoon by Dik Browne that featured a Viking sailor and his complaining homebound wife. "I don't mind your being a Viking," says the wife, "but you're never home, you're always sailing off to some place. Why don't you work closer to home. Is that too much to ask?"

"If I did my work closer to home," responds Hagar, "they'd put me in jail."

John was Robbi's modern-day Viking, a strapping thirty-one-year-old with dirty-blond hair and a full brown beard. He was strong but not muscular, with a winning smile and a ready hand to extend to those less fortunate than himself.

The IRA offered John the focus his life had lacked, a purpose for living and, if necessary, for dying. The *Valhalla*'s voyage merged John's genuine zeal for Irish freedom with the exciting underworld of smuggling, guns, and death.

As soon as they cleared the harbor, John rolled up the maps of Georges Bank and put them away. Anderson watched as John took a computer reading from the navigation satellite orbiting overhead. He read the numbers off of the NAVSAT display and punched them into the Loran navigation unit. Unfolding a piece of paper, he carefully entered the coordinates of their destination: the middle of nowhere one hundred miles off the Irish coast. The *Valhalla*'s powerful engines could make almost twelve knots. John predicted that they would reach the rendezvous in ten or twelve days.

Once the destination coordinates were entered, the computer marked their exact location and determined their precise course. John copied the longitude and latitude of the rendezvous location onto a calendar hanging nearby. He and Anderson would take turns navigating by the Loran radar to this point.

"Next stop, Ireland," said Anderson.

John answered with a boyish grin and went to his bunk below to rest before his watch at the helm.

He settled in for the long ride with Robert Kee's *The Green Flag*, a history of Irish nationalism, and Padraig O'Malley's *Uncivil Wars*. His broad literary tastes spoke well to his dual nature. He was the tough soldier who fit right in with the IRA's underworld and never let a slight, real or imagined, pass unanswered; he was also the well-read young man, full of intelligent enthusiasm, determined to behold good in the world, often where there was none to be seen.

Meanwhile, Sean Crawley attended to his own duties. In the compartments below deck, there were seven tons of guns and state-of-the-art electronic gear that John had ordered for eavesdropping on British communications—umbrella mikes to pick up British military conferences at long range, devices to tap police communications, and countersurveillance equipment to detect British electronic penetration efforts. During the voyage, Sean inventoried the arms cache in a red spiral notebook: seventy-three new assault rifles, stolen from an Ohio National Guard armory; fifty-two older military weapons; twenty-three miscellaneous guns stolen from homes in the Boston area and bought from thieves; a .30-caliber M-1 carbine; a .50-caliber Browning heavy machine gun; and thirteen weapons Murray had purchased legally that summer.

The stockpile included M-16 rifles, the standard issue of the U.S. Army; Colt AR-15s, the civilian version of the M-16; and Heckler and Koch assault rifles. All were shorn of traceable serial numbers and modified for automatic fire. There were also single-barrel breach-loading shotguns, Smith and Wesson "Dirty Harry" revolvers, hardware that would adapt the Browning machine gun for antiaircraft fire, and seventy-one thousand rounds of ammunition, suitable for everything from the machine gun to the rifles.

Sean counted Aimpoint electronic rifle sights, useful for snipers, and eleven bulletproof vests—the same type of body armor used by British troops and the officers of the Royal Ulster Constabulary. One of the vests had been shot full of holes by various kinds of bullets. There were circles drawn around each hole with notations about the caliber and distance that produced each result—a hands-on guide to the most deadly ammunition against British forces. The shipment also included a large assortment of gun cases, military webbing and belts, spare parts, weapons pouches, thousands of ammunition clips, additional night and telescopic sights, and waterproof ammo cans.

After taking inventory of the weapons and matériel, Sean repacked them in assorted carrying cases, steamer trunks, fish boxes, cardboard boxes, wooden crates, and bags and stored them below.

Sean was partial to explosives—a hobby he picked up during his training as a demolitions expert for the Navy SEALs. He carefully laid out grenades and sealed plastic envelopes containing the construction explosive cordite in neat rows in the *Valhalla*'s cramped quarters.

"What the hell are you doing?" asked John.

Sean assured him that without detonators, the black Korean fragmentation grenades and explosive charges were all but harmless.

"These are the suckers to worry about," he said, opening another of the wooden packing crates. Sean reached in and picked up a Redeye surface-to-air antiaircraft missile, a deadly shoulder-fired guided missile with an infrared homing device. Pointed at the hot exhaust of an enemy plane, the little Redeye can wreak havoc in the air. The Soviets learned this lesson firsthand in Afghanistan, where antigovernment forces had been covertly supplied with the weapon by Washington. Sean had some friends in the Green Berets who had stolen a few for him—and for the IRA.

Sean had made sure to bring along a stack of manuals and firearms literature, including a U.S. Army technical primer on heavy machine guns. As part of developing the IRA's new military strategy, Sean had prepared a handwritten syllabus and timetable headed "Twenty-one day column training." Sean, the former Navy SEAL, and Pat Nee, a decorated Marine Corps veteran who had seen a lot of action in Vietnam, were planning to train a large group of IRA soldiers in advanced military techniques—reconnaissance, surveillance, commando attacks—at a full-scale training facility that they would help establish in one of the Republic's border counties. The IRA would use this training facility and the weapons smuggled aboard the *Valhalla* to prepare the attacks that would follow the assassination operation against the British prime minister and her cabinet.

Measured against the weapons available to the British, the arsenal inventoried in Sean's notebook wasn't terribly impressive. Still, it represented one of the largest shipments ever assembled by the IRA and heralded a marked change in IRA tactics from its isolated ambushes and acts of terror to a more conventional, and threatening, military strategy. If the security John had devised was effective, the weapons aboard the *Valhalla* promised to be the first of a series of arms dispatched to the IRA from the Boston pipeline.

On the evening of September 20, 1984, barely one week after the *Valhalla* began its journey across the blustery Atlantic, Joe Murray, his pregnant wife Sue, Pat Nee and his girlfriend, and another couple left Boston's Logan Airport on Aer Lingus flight 116, bound for Dublin. Because of the DEA's ongoing suspicions about Murray's involvement in the drug trade, his name had long been on the watch list plugged into the airline's reservations and passenger-manifest computers. Murray's departure for Shannon Airport was noted by U.S. Customs, which lacked the resources to follow up with surveillance. The Dublin authorities, to whom Murray's IRA sympathies were no secret, took no notice of his journey, perhaps because Murray and his wife managed to slip into Ireland without filling out any customs declarations. As far as the Irish knew, Joe Murray had never entered their country.

Once in Ireland, the group remained together only briefly. Nee, his companion, and the other couple left for a tour of the countryside: Murray and his wife stayed near Shannon Airport. Murray had arranged to meet Martin Ferris, a fisherman from the nearby port of Fenit. Ferris was also the Provo commander for the southwest region, including counties Cork and Kerry, where the arms would come ashore aboard the *Marita Ann*. At their meeting, Murray confirmed the *Valhalla*'s imminent arrival. Ferris, the IRA's top man in the region, would himself escort Murray to the *Marita Ann*. This time, it seemed, security would be maintained.

After meeting with Murray, Ferris approached Michael Browne, the skipper of the *Marita Ann*, and told him that his boat was needed for an upcoming IRA operation. Browne agreed to bring along his two crew members who, for security reasons, would be told that the boat was sailing to Carrigaholt, near the mouth of the Shannon River in County Clare, for general repairs to the hull.

Here, the plan John had so diligently conceived began to go awry.

Shortly after arriving in Ireland, Joe Murray nervously announced that his wife Sue was suddenly having trouble with her pregnancy. For Joe, who had already lost a son to illness, the health of his wife and baby took precedence over any allegiance to John, who depended upon him to be on the *Marita Ann*, or to the IRA, which had pushed him into the operation in the first place.

To the astonishment of the group, Joe announced that he was taking his wife back to America for a checkup immediately, and refused to listen to any arguments. Pat Nee could go ahead and pick up the trucks as planned, Ferris could escort the *Marita Ann* to the *Valhalla* by himself. Joe did not care.

Murray and his ailing wife returned to Boston on September 24 aboard Aer Lingus Flight 117. Murray once again managed to evade all customs and passport controls by slipping through a side door, leaving no official record that he had ever left Boston. Murray didn't like paper tails. They were bad for business.

Before he left Ireland, Murray gave the IRA's Martin Ferris the rendezvous coordinates that John had tried so zealously to safeguard and arranged for Ferris to take charge of the off-loading operations aboard the *Marita Ann*. Nee, rather than oversee the ocean transfer as planned, was told to stay in his Dublin hotel and wait for word of the boat's return.

At three in the morning on Tuesday, September 25, the *Marita Ann* left the port of Fenit with Browne, Ferris, and two unsuspecting crewmen, already asleep for the night, and a couple of fugitives who were to be transferred to the *Valhalla*.

When the crewmen woke the next morning, Ferris told them that they weren't headed for Carrigaholt but were instead going on an IRA operation. Ferris didn't explain the nature of the operation, nor did the frightened crewmen think it in their interest to know. He said that for security reasons they had to be brought along; it would arouse suspicion if the boat left Fenit without its regular crew. Ferris promised that they were in no danger and told them to keep their mouths shut, stay out of sight below decks, and say nothing when they returned to port. Whatever the crew's doubts, they were in no position to complain.

The *Marita Ann* was out of port less than twelve hours when it was stopped dead by engine problems. The ship drifted listlessly as Browne and Ferris worked all of Tuesday afternoon and on through the night to repair the engine's gear box.

Late on the afternoon of Thursday, September 27, the two vessels approached their scheduled ocean rendezvous in the swollen, choppy seas. A North Atlantic storm was brewing, and the swells were already ten feet high and rising. Anticipating confusion over the ship's identity, Ferris had draped a white canvas cloth, on which "IRA" was painted in red letters almost a foot tall, over the *Marita Ann*'s port side. Anderson, a veteran of many such meetings, could well have done without the crude and amateurish display. He had already picked up the *Marita Ann*'s radar signal—a solitary beacon in an otherwise empty sea, 120 miles west of Kerry in the Porcupine Bank fishing area. For security purposes, the two ships were to maintain radio silence throughout the arms transfer. Even though the *Marita Ann* was flagrantly advertising its origins, John didn't want to give IRA trackers from British intelligence any opportunity to detect their presence electronically.

When the ships were within fifty yards of each other, John took out his binoculars to search for Murray among those standing on the *Marita Ann*'s swaying deck. Joe's presence would be John's first and best indication that the Irish end of the operation was proceeding smoothly. And, John thought, it would redeem Murray, the greedy drug runner, as a true IRA patriot.

John scanned the ship time and time again, scrutinizing the faces of the men on board. "Where the hell is that bastard Murray?" he muttered to himself. "He promised he would be there to meet us." John couldn't believe it, but Joe, despite their arrangement, was nowhere to be found.

"That bastard!" John shouted in fury. This wasn't the first time that Murray had bailed out of a tight situation. He had beaten a drug rap back in Boston and managed to stay at least one step ahead of the alphabet soup of federal agencies trying to jail him. John knew Murray shared his ability to outsmart the paunchy flatfoots and pencil-pushers trying to trip up men who challenged the system. But he resented Murray's instincts for self-preservation when it came to walking out on the IRA—and double-crossing him.

John prized loyalty above all other values. In the world of daring and intrigue he had fashioned, John had cast Murray as a man of action and commitment to the cause of Irish freedom. John knew that Murray ran drugs and did not doubt that he was a killer as well. But he had always balanced these activities against his trust in Joe's pledge to the IRA. After all, it was through Joe that John had discovered his true calling as a soldier in the struggle for a united Ireland. Joe had slowly introduced John to the operations of the Boston IRA, entrusting him with more and more power.

Murray's absence undermined the emotional obligation so critical to John, who was prepared to sacrifice all for the cause. When he realized that Murray had backed out of the operation at its most critical moment, John was forced to question not only Murray's commitment, but his own as well.

Everything John knew about undercover operations demanded that the transfer be cancelled. He immediately decided that Murray's failure to accompany the *Marita Ann* had compromised the entire operation. The *Valhalla*'s load would have to be dumped at sea and arrangements made for another transfer under more secure circumstances.

The crew aboard the *Marita Ann* had to be informed, but even now, John didn't want to break radio silence. He told Anderson to bring the *Valhalla* to within thirty feet or so of the *Marita Ann*, which by this time was pitching wildly in the fury of the storm. As it grew darker, John readied the *Valhalla*'s white ten-foot dinghy, attached a safety line to its transom, and dropped it over the side. He started the motor and, towing the safety line behind him, expertly maneuvered through the treacherous swells to the *Marita Ann*. John planned to leave the dinghy on the *Marita Ann* and be towed back on the safety line to the *Valhalla*.

Once John was aboard, Ferris informed him of Murray's last-minute change in plans. John still could not accept any excuse for Murray's absence. But he wanted desperately to see his faith and commitment vindicated, and so he let Ferris and Browne convince him that the transfer could still proceed in safety.

Fiasco at Sea

By this time, the sky was completely black. Both ships were running without any lights, and the storm was howling. The seas were incredible. Thirty-foot swells made it impossible for the two ships, pitching like corks in a tank, to draw alongside each other. They needed to get close enough to use the hydraulic arm fixed on the *Marita Ann*'s starboard side to lift sea nets filled with weapons off the *Valhalla* and carry them across to the *Marita Ann*. But even if they did manage to go gunnel to gunnel, the raging action of the sea would smash the boats against one another unmercifully, leaving on each vessel a trail of paint chips as easily identifiable as a fingerprint. In the calm seas John had hoped for, such a maneuver would have posed no problem at all. But in the white-crested swells of the stormy mid-Atlantic, the steel-hulled *Valhalla* would most probably put a life-threatening gash in the *Marita Ann*'s wooden hull.

Despite the risk, they tried to come alongside only to pull away quickly when the two vessels nearly smashed into each other.

Once John had committed himself to the transfer, there was no stopping it, despite his better judgment. The arms delivery had to take place—here and now—on the open ocean, under the protective cover of the blackened sky. But how was John to move seven tons of weapons in total darkness across a raging sea?

John McIntyre excelled when circumstances forced him to think on his feet. But that night's mission was a severe test of both his planning abilities and the seamanship skills of those aboard both vessels. The first victim of their predicament was the plan to maintain radio silence. There was simply no other way that John, still aboard the *Marita Ann*, could communicate his orders to Anderson over the raging storm.

John ordered the bows of both boats to be pointed dead into the violent, cresting waves. Anderson and Browne maneuvered their boats to within thirty yards of each other, close enough to enable John to attach a long, steel cable to his safety line, which Sean, on the *Valhalla*, hauled back aboard. Coupled to the cable was a rig that John had devised: a block and tackle joined to a cargo net.

Each vessel had huge crane booms mounted on both sides of its bridge. When used for fishing, the boats' dragging nets would be dropped into the water from these booms, which could swing far out over the water; the nets would then be cranked over the stern on the huge spool near the aft fish-holding tank.

Tonight there were no fish to catch—just guns. A heavy cable with a pulley attached was strung between the booms on each ship, and a separate towing line was put in place to guide the pulley from one ship to the other.

John courageously offered himself as the first load to be drawn from one boat to the other, twenty feet above the raging seas. As the sea rolled, John crawled into the net and gave the signal for the *Valhalla* to draw him slowly across. Had the captains aboard the two vessels faltered, John would have been plunged into the churning water. Once in the sea, the net that had cradled John above the water would have frustrated his every effort to escape. With his optimism and passion for daring, John ignored this danger.

The system worked flawlessly. Once on board, John and Sean loaded boxes of munitions into the cargo net, which they then attached to the pulley. John signalled the men on the *Marita Ann* to draw the loaded net over the undulating sea, using one of the *Marita Ann*'s powerful hydraulic winches. The net safely negotiated the span between the two boats and was then lowered into the main hold of the *Marita Ann*, where the two shanghaied crewmen unloaded the guns. When they finished, the empty net was sent back to the *Valhalla* for another load.

The transfer was a tricky business. Both captains had to

fight wind and turbulent waves to hold the boats far enough apart to keep the heavy cargo net out of the water, but not so far that the cables spanning them would snap. Throughout the night, Anderson was forced to bark brief radio instructions to the *Marita Ann* to keep the boats working in tandem.

The morning sun was rising as the last of the wooden crates was safely guided into the hold of the *Marita Ann*. Ferris ordered the two IRA soldiers on the run from the British into the net and watched as they drifted over the frothing ocean and were dropped unceremoniously onto the *Valhalla's* deck.

John watched as Sean climbed into the net for the return trip to Ireland. As he was lifted off of the deck, Sean pulled the blue military intelligence cap out of his jacket and waved it. He had stolen John's father's hat out of the sea bag.

"For luck," yelled Sean as he swung out over the ocean.

The morning had brought sunlight but no respite from the blustering storm. The men aboard the two ships had worked through the night to ferry the cache of weapons and supplies. They had successfully accomplished the most demanding part of their mission and were anxious to return to their respective ports, an ocean apart.

The two vessels signaled their farewells. The men were just about to dismantle the rigging John had devised when they heard the whoosh of a low-flying jet directly overhead. John knew enough about military reconnaissance aircraft to identify the low-flying plane as an RAF Nimrod—equipped with over-the-horizon radar, state-of-the-art electronics, and most probably a high-resolution look-down camera mounted on its fuselage.

Until that moment, John hadn't considered the need to guard against surveillance from the air. The *Valhalla* was an easy mark. Its name was painted in marine red on both sides of the bow and across the transom, which also carried the name of the ship's home port—Ipswich, Massachusetts. The *Marita Ann* had covered the name on its transom with white canvas, but it inexplicably still displayed the IRA sign tacked onto its port side.

Even if the British could now identify the boats, thought John, they had no way of knowing who was aboard them. Luckily, everyone on the *Valhalla* was still wearing the ski masks and watch caps donned the evening before to guard against the cold. The crew aboard the *Marita Ann* weren't so lucky—or so smart. John screamed in anger when he saw some of the bare-faced passengers staring directly at the plane.

"Don't look up," he yelled, but the noise of the plane and the storm drowned out his cry.

As the plane banked to make another pass over the ships, John watched in disbelief as one of the men aboard the *Marita Ann*, he could not tell who, fumbled with the straps of a Redeye missile while hoisting it onto his shoulder. As the plane roared overhead, he fired wildly. The telltale smoke trailed up from the deck of the *Marita Ann* as the missile itself streaked harmlessly past its target, hundreds of feet away from the jet's side.

Fishing boats don't usually carry heat-seeking missiles, but panic-stricken gunrunners for underground movements like the IRA do. The *Marita Ann* might just as well have fired off a signal flare announcing "IRA GUNS HERE." The pilot dipped and banked suddenly before racing eastward to his base somewhere in the British Isles.

Like all previous IRA shipments, the *Valhalla*'s mission had been compromised. On or before Monday, September 24, British intelligence had been apprised of the *Marita Ann*'s imminent departure. For political reasons, it was decided to let the Irish take the lead in intercepting the arms shipment.

Fiasco at Sea

As the *Marita Ann* prepared to leave Fenit, thirty heavily armed members of the Irish national police assembled at the Haulbowline Naval Base in Cork Harbor on Ireland's southern coast. This special force, armed with UZI submachine guns, boarded two small, fast Irish Navy vessels, the *Emer* and *Aisling*. The two vessels were not informed of their mission but were ordered to sail westward around the Irish coast and to wait at a specified position concealed between the Great and Little Skellig rocks outside of Ballinskelligs Bay. From Monday evening onward, they had remained near the Skelligs, the men tense with anticipation and impatient for the mystery ship's arrival.

The Irish lacked long-range radar, so Britain offered the tracking services of the Nimrod, usually on the prowl for Soviet submarines in the North Atlantic. The Nimrod could transmit up-to-the-minute reports on the locations of the two vessels as they approached the rendezvous. The plane had tracked the *Marita Ann* since its departure from Fenit and had monitored and taped portions of the conversation between Anderson and Browne during the night of the arms transfer.

When it became light enough the next morning to take pictures, the Nimrod made its approach. The pilot remained out of the range of small-arms fire, but flew low enough to snap identifying pictures of the *Valhalla*. The heat-seeking missile had spooked him, but as the *Marita Ann* lumbered through the continuing gale towards the coast with its seven tons of weapons on board, the Nimrod, now out of sight, continued to radio its progress via intelligence channels to the Irish.

All day Friday she sailed unmolested, the canvas emblazoned with the word "IRA" still thoughtlessly hung over the side for all to see. At 11:20 PM on Friday, September 28, the *Emer*'s navigating officer picked up a radar contact on his screen. The ship's commander instructed him to plot the

21

course of the boat, which was now 8.6 miles west of Great Skellig Rock. Aboard the *Marita Ann*, Crawley, Ferris, and the two crewmen were walking around the deck smoking cigarettes and enjoying the seasonably warm night air.

Forty minutes later, the *Marita Ann* was still 2.6 miles west of the Skelligs, but its navigation lights had become visible to the *Emer*. Within minutes, the *Marita Ann* entered Ireland's territorial waters, which extend three miles from shore. Now she was fair game for the Irish Navy. At eleven minutes past midnight, the *Emer*, operating without running lights, proceeded at full speed to intercept the vessel, still about three miles away.

When the *Emer* had come to within one-half mile of the *Marita Ann*, the officers signaled the trawler to stop, flashing a signal lamp and sounding the *Emer*'s siren. The captain personally made a call on VHF radio ordering the IRA vessel to halt. But rather than heave to, the *Marita Ann* altered course in an apparent effort to escape.

As the swifter *Emer* continued to close in, its captain picked up the VHF microphone and broadcast, "This is the Irish naval vessel *Emer*, Long Eireannac *Emer*. Stop your vessel."

At the same moment, the ship's executive officer was calling over a megaphone, "Stop your vessel, stop your vessel, or we will open fire."

The *Emer*, now only two hundred feet away, illuminated the *Marita Ann* with strong search lights. Still, she tried to maneuver away in zigs and zags, an impossible task for the run-down trawler even in the best of circumstances. The *Emer* continued to close. It was now only twenty feet from its prey. It fired four warning shots—tracer ammunition that illuminated the night sky—across the *Marita Ann*'s bow.

Only then did Ferris concede defeat and order Browne to cut the engines. The *Marita Ann* was now 2.2 miles northwest of Great Skellig Lighthouse and less than 2 miles from the Irish coast. It was almost half past twelve.

Ferris ordered everyone on board to the stern of the boat. He told them to keep their mouths shut, to ask only for a solicitor. He repeated that they weren't to say anything until they had seen a solicitor.

They were waiting when a party of the Irish Navy and the heavily armed officers of the Garda Siochana, the Irish national police force, boarded the *Marita Ann*.

A quick survey of the ship by the Irish authorities revealed the arms mission. Bulletproof vests were found in the captain's cabin, and a loaded FN rifle was found under a blanket on a bunk. On the lower deck, officers found a box of hand grenades, a firearms manual, and Sean's inventory of the cache scrawled in an American notebook with its price tag intact. A quick look into the main hold revealed the firearms and ammunition.

At 12:44 AM on September 29, the vessel's passengers were arrested under Ireland's Offenses Against the State Act. Crawley and one crewman were put aboard the *Aisling*, while Ferris and the other crewman were transferred to the *Emer*. Browne remained with his boat for the trip to port. The *Marita Ann*, however, soon broke down completely and was unable to continue under its own power. It was towed by the *Aisling* to Haulbowline Naval Base, where it arrived some hours later. The biggest arms shipment in IRA history had gone bust. No one involved realized that the mission had been compromised by a spy within the IRA's own ranks.

The capture was big news in Ireland. Sinn Fein, the political wing of the Provisional IRA, declared the IRA's efforts would not be impeded by the seizure. The organization blamed the Dublin government for continuously "postponing Ireland's freedom by acting as agents for Britain."

Garret FitzGerald, Ireland's prime minister, replied that

"Many lives of Irish people and indeed others may have been saved by this.

"There are still people in the United States," he lamented, "who, failing to comprehend the situation in this country, are willing to give aid to purchase and send arms to murder Irish people, including our police and armed forces."

As soon as he had spotted the Nimrod, John had ordered Anderson to cut the lines between the two ships. The *Marita Ann* was on its own. From that first moment, John knew the arms he had so carefully assembled and transported would never reach their intended destination.

Anderson didn't need to be told what to do. He cranked up the *Valhalla*'s engine to top speed and made for points west—as far away from Ireland, the *Marita Ann*, and the RAF as the *Valhalla* could take him.

The going was tough. Daylight had merely given form to the storm that had raged furiously throughout the night. The *Valhalla* pitched and yawed frantically as it plunged into moving walls of water and spray.

John was up on the bridge with Anderson. Down below, the pallor of the IRA fugitives had turned from white to a sickly greenish yellow. Already exhausted by the long night's work aboard the *Marita Ann*, these landlubbers were now terrified by the crazed violence of the sea.

Hour after hour, the waves attacked the steel-plated wheelhouse. John was beyond exhaustion. The exhilaration he had felt as he saw the last of the arms being stored aboard the *Marita Ann* had given way to the pain of failure. Now, his battle against the elements overwhelmed any consideration of deeds past. Every atom of his consciousness was focused on finding a way to outlast the storm.

Suddenly, a rogue wave came out of nowhere, towering over the bow. Crashing on the deck, the torrent hurled itself against the three-inch-thick safety glass John had installed in the oblong windows of the wheelhouse. Two of these bullet-proof tempered-glass plates were blown inward; sea water rushed through the openings. The bridge began to flood. John quickly turned on the salt-water pumps and, with Anderson, quickly covered the shattered windows with plywood. Miraculously, the Loran radar system was not shorted out by the sea water. But the rogue wave had maimed the old *Valhalla*; another would finish her off for sure.

John and Anderson worked tirelessly through the night to keep the *Valhalla*'s overworked pumps operating. The water that surged aboard was dangerously unnecessary ballast; the boat could founder if another wave hit. Luckily, the rogue was a final, defiant gasp of a now-exhausted storm. As dawn broke, twenty-four hours after the *Valhalla* had been spotted by the Nimrod, the storm had blown itself out. John woke from an uneasy hour's sleep to the clanging of loose rigging and the familiar, reassuring hum of the ship's diesel engine chugging its way homeward. He roused his sore body, bruised by a night of tossing against bulkheads and pipes, and made his way to the bridge to relieve Anderson. Bob was too tired to speak, and John was too concerned about their voyage to notice. He mechanically noted the navigational readouts on the calendar and took the wheel. As John looked around him at the tangle of lines and debris littering the deck, his heart sank. The disastrous reality of the last two days crashed down upon him.

The moment John had seen the Nimrod, he felt in his gut that Joe Murray had intentionally exposed the operation. John had been utterly and completely betrayed by the man he considered both friend and counselor.

Except for John's father, Joe Murray was the only man whose authority John had ever respected. Now Joe had sold the Feds the *Valhalla* and its crew, probably in return for favors connected to the Boston drug trade. Murray's treachery was John's only explanation for Joe's convenient absence and the sudden appearance of the British spy plane.

Anderson agreed, and for the first time told John McIntyre how his friend Joe Murray had ruthlessly climbed to power in the Mob, cutting down anyone in his way.

John said he didn't believe it, but he was fooling himself. At first, he refused to accept that the Boston Commander of the Provos had a secret life as a major mafioso, but what Anderson was saying had the ring of truth. John had to admit Anderson should know since he smuggled drugs for a living. Anderson described Murray's safe house on Marlborough street in Boston's prestigious Back Bay, where stacks of counterfeit bills were hidden behind plaster, and told John about Murray's liquor store that delivered kilos of cocaine in brown paper bags. John had heard similar stories from Brendan Kelly, whose brother had died on the *Sea Mist,* one of Frankie LePere's drug boats. Brendan had refused to go on the *Valhalla* and warned him to beware of Murray. Maybe John did not want to admit the truth then, maybe he did not want to know, and never asked the right questions when he agreed to smuggle pot for Murray. It all seemed so exciting then, not to mention it paid well. He had no one to blame but himself. He would deal with Murray later; right now he had more urgent business.

The *Valhalla* had survived, scarred but not beaten. John knew that he, Anderson, and the IRA fugitives would be lucky to get out of their troubles as easily. John assumed that British intelligence had sent clear photos of the *Valhalla* to the U.S. Coast Guard and perhaps to the FBI as well. London had been clamoring for their American counterparts to demonstrate more zeal in the pursuit of America's IRA sympathizers; the *Valhalla* offered such an opportunity. John knew that the ship had been totally compromised. There would be no easy way to talk himself out of this predicament. A greeting party of self-satisfied Feds would probably intercept the *Valhalla* and her crew even before they reached shore.

But what if the *Valhalla* never made it to shore? John had no trouble convincing Anderson that their best chance of evading capture was to scuttle the boat in the deep water off Georges Bank and to make for the Canadian coast in the well-outfitted survival rafts John had stored in the *Valhalla*'s hold. But John and Bob were both professional seamen, more at home in the brine and salt air than on land. Their two passengers had never been out in so much as a rowboat on a lake before this maritime adventure. These seasick souls thought it was sheer lunacy to abandon the *Valhalla* for a couple of tiny rubber rafts. John's entreaties fell on deaf ears. At one point, the armed fugitives threatened to get nasty. John had enough problems without an uneven gunfight on the open seas.

John then suggested that they activate the cover story they invented before leaving Gloucester. The *Valhalla* would stay out at sea, fishing for a few weeks off Georges Bank. It would mingle with the huge fishing fleets hailing from Boston and Halifax before selling its catch in Newfoundland. There, John and Anderson would sell the boat and take leave of their queasy passengers. The Feds certainly would know about the *Valhalla* and its role in the arms transfer, but John wanted to believe they had no way of knowing who was on her when the exchange took place.

The plan didn't get far with the *Valhalla*'s surly IRA outlaws. After their introduction to maritime sport and the vagaries of autumn weather, they wanted to plant their feet on terra firma as quickly as possible. They refused to help repair the storm-damaged rigging or conserve the ship's limited water supplies by taking fewer showers. These men had no intention of hauling fish for weeks on end. They left little doubt that they would use the weapons they had to force Anderson to return immediately to shore.

John was angered by the attitude of these hardened IRA heroes. The IRA had always had the strictest discipline and the tightest security. Yet, they lost each battle. How foolish John had been to think that he alone could improve the Provos' shoddy record. The vision of the Redeye missile flying recklessly from the deck of the *Marita Ann* played over and over in his mind. Even if the IRA had received the guns aboard the *Marita Ann*, he decided, they would always be defeated in combat by the British, who had better spy networks and shorter supply lines. The Provos would never be able to defeat the British by force of arms.

Sitting on his bunk belowdecks, John despaired at his gullibility, which would almost certainly cost him a long prison term. John sensed that he had become a victim as well as an unwitting player in the latest IRA paramilitary farce. His enthusiasm for the IRA's military strategy vanished. The double-dealing and incompetence he had experienced since leaving Gloucester less than one month before filled him with regrets.

John pulled out a three-inch-wide notepad and tried to record his remorse and anger.

"I wish I had never made this trip," he wrote. He brooded over the armchair patriots who filled the Irish bars in Southie and Charlestown—men whose idea of patriotism was crooning an IRA ballad in an inebriated swoon—and about his blind faith in the cowardly Murray.

"Every time I go into an Irish bar, I know why it takes them so long to win this, just by the way they love their Irish songs. They romanticize this war," John wrote, unaware that he was guilty of the same offense.

He thought of the German marching songs—the ballad of the panzer grenadiers and the submariners' hymn—that he and his best friend Chuck had listened to when they were kids. If only the IRA could be imbued with some of that

German spirit, instead of the weepy, melancholy ballads that were played at Murray's pub.

"I wish [Chuck] would let them listen to their German marching songs," he scribbled, "then get this goddamn war over with fast."

But even as he scrawled these words, John had decided on another, less militant strategy. The shock of Murray's apparent betrayal had destroyed his romantic faith in the armed revolutionary struggle. What the IRA needed, John impetuously concluded, was an entirely new approach to fighting the British. And John, with the same enthusiasm that first convinced him of the necessity for gunrunning, now decided that he would lead a propaganda offensive for the freedom of Northern Ireland.

The *Valhalla* fiasco, John wrote, "does not have to be a complete loss. I wish there were enough sympathetic Irishmen on Madison [Avenue]. Pressure to make this trip into a crusade for the Irish people.

"Newspeople have to do it," he wrote, with all the conviction of the convert. "What a way to win a revolution. Sympathy, sympathy, sympathy, the only way."

John would exploit the notoriety gained from his role in the botched arms smuggling to speak with authority about the senselessness of the IRA's preoccupation with armed struggle. He saw himself winning support for Ireland's cause among Boston's Irish Brahmins and the elected politicians like Congressman Joe Moakley and Senator Ted Kennedy who had always condemned the violent ways of the IRA.

"I hope I can run fast enough to bring the Joes [Moakley] around and the Teds [Kennedy]," John wrote. According to the simple plan John penned on the high seas, the American public would soon see the justice of the Irish claims. They would convince Washington to pressure Britain into giving up Northern Ireland.

John had set out from Gloucester with a cache of guns to

support the IRA's military campaign against the British. As he neared the American continent four weeks later, he had transformed himself from armed revolutionary into propagandist. His newfound enthusiasm was perhaps no more realistic than his original zeal. Still, it offered him hope, a plan. John would not abandon his bedrock devotion to the cause. It was the slender thread that kept intact John's all-important emotional commitment to the IRA. This commitment was the only thing that could justify the risks he had taken.

"I pray," he wrote in his last entry, "that I haven't made this trip to have lost everything." He thought of his American countrymen, ambivalent to the war that had gone on too long. "Pray my idea will move them for Ireland."

Before John could argue the cause of Irish freedom to America, the *Valhalla* had to be brought safely—and secretly—to port. This was the only option the ocean-weary IRA fugitives would permit. John and Anderson agreed that the best plan was the most audacious. They would dock where the Coast Guard and Joe Murray would least expect them.

On Saturday evening, October 13, the *Valhalla* mingled with the fishing fleet as it headed toward Boston Harbor. After they passed Boston Light, the city opened up before the exhausted crew. As they entered President's Road, the main channel through the harbor, John watched anxiously for signs of a Coast Guard boarding party.

2

~~~~~~

BURDEN OF TRUTH

The *Valhalla* was the first love of John's life. Not the sea-battered survivor that he and Anderson abandoned at the Northern Avenue pier, but the prim sailing dinghy with the gleaming hull and varnished thwarts that John had owned as a boy of ten.

John grew up on Squantum's Ocean Avenue, moving from a small home to a larger one down the street when his father's salary as a vending-machine salesman allowed. Neither his father, John, nor his mother, Emily, were sailors. But John didn't need their example to spark his attraction to the sea. In Squantum, a small peninsular town wedged between the salt marshes and the ocean just south of Boston, the ever-present water charmed and captured the energies of the adventurous young boy.

Today, like other Massachusetts towns linked tenuously to the mainland, Squantum has let the frenetic pace of the city and nearby suburbs pass it by. Kids abandon their bikes on the sidewalk outside the corner grocery store, whose owner stands behind the counter displaying candy and the latest edition of the *Herald* and the *Boston Globe* and knows all of his young customers by name.

Even within this time-arrested world, John lived on what

the local real estate agency advertises as "the sleepy side of town," a mixed neighborhood of professionals, lobstermen, and working-class families. Luxurious houses, once summer cottages for the rich, sit side by side with cramped, incongruously shaped dwellings which lack an architect's practiced touch. These varied houses lend an entirely accidental yet authentic quality to the neighborhood. John's house was somewhere in between, a comfortable two-story white colonial on a narrow lot, with tall stairs leading up to the front porch. The lawn, a well-tended strip of grass, holds a few nautical decorations.

A short path from the end of John's dead-end street leads to the harbor. It boasts a small beach littered with the implements of the fishing trade. Small prams, their scuffed bottoms turned to the sky, lie strewn along the high-water mark; lobster traps are piled absentmindedly along the shore.

Every day after school, John, with his best friend Chuck trailing behind, would head straight for his backyard to work on the *Valhalla*. There were no shortcuts to readying a wooden boat for the water, even one as small as that little dinghy. John devoted himself to making the boat seaworthy, scraping and sanding the bottom before caulking between the wooden planking, repairing and replacing brass fittings, and, when she was ready, carefully painting the name *Valhalla* on the bow. Here he learned the basic skills that, at only ten, gave him an unusual confidence on the water.

John waited for a gale to come up off the Squantum beach before taking the *Valhalla* out on her maiden voyage. Chuck was waiting by the garage when John's mother, Emily, arrived. When Chuck told her where John was, Emily raced down to the swollen ocean, now a blanket of whitecaps. Amid the cresting swells, she spotted a small red sail. She waved repeatedly for John to come ashore.

John was alone on the water and having the time of his life. He loved a storm and relished the thrill of challenging the elements. Emily once remarked that the violence of an ocean squall brought out the opposite of fear in him. Where others felt only a healthy, instinctive apprehension, John sensed in the restless sea the liberating opportunity for innocent adventure and daring heroism.

When John finally brought the boat in, Emily greeted her soaked but otherwise intact son with angry reproaches and a stern admonition never to repeat the escapade. His father, on the other hand, couldn't repress an approving smile when he told John not to worry his mother with such antics. John would not soon forget the memory of this day or the secret understanding sealed with his proud father.

John was an avid reader of adventure stories and military history, his imagination fired by the books he discovered in his father's large library. The islands and open water along the Massachusetts coast became the stage where John, a wiry boy with blond hair, acted out his youthful fantasies.

When he was no more than seven, John had become convinced that America was first discovered by the Vikings. For weekends on end, John led both parents, shovels in hand, to nearby Moon Island to dig for evidence of Viking colonies. A few years later, after reading one of his father's many books, John decided that Viking treasure was buried on Long Island, connected to Squantum by a causeway that crossed Moon Island. He convinced his neighborhood friends to set off on a treasure hunt, and together they dug for Viking graves among the cavernous World War II gun emplacements that dotted the island. As they searched, John told the boys about the Norse legend that only those Vikings who died a hero's death in combat could enter Valhalla, the warrior's heaven. Among the island dunes, the children played Viking war games, shouting "Valhalla" at they charged their imaginary enemies. No Viking relics were ever unearthed, but it was here, among the debris from the army's training exercises against Nazi invasion, that John began his collection of spent shells.

As a boy, John rarely cried; he shared this trait with his mother. Emily, a strong stoic woman, similarly resembled her own mother, whose stern, Hepburnesque portrait occupied a place of honor in the Ocean Avenue dining room. From John's earliest years, the water and the history-filled islands of Boston Harbor put him on the road to manhood. He loved to work on his boat or go sailing.

In school, John excelled at subjects that interested him—chemistry, math, and physics. His early love for reading continued into his teens. Books about the American Civil War, the U.S. Navy and World War II filled the family bookshelves. When they were children, he and Chuck collected World War II souvenirs, coins, and milk glass. In high school, their collections gave way to boats, old cars, and girls.

John had a good time in Cub Scouts, Boy Scouts, and Sea Scouts. He was like any other kid in Squantum. He was book smart, but there was also something of the daredevil in him—and he never shrank from a fight. Bloody noses and the hazards embraced by young boys anxious to be men were common currency in Squantum. And in this scrip, John was no poorer than any of his peers.

As a young teenager, he engaged in a fair share of pranks. But he never did any real harm. John's home became the neighborhood clubhouse; Mr. McIntyre had a full repertoire of songs, jokes, and war stories that fascinated John's friends.

The summer before John's senior year in high school, his family made a five-week tour of Europe. It was the first time that his parents had been to Europe since the fifties, and they were anxious to get reacquainted with Emily's family and their many old friends.

Emily had been born in Germany in 1928. She was a happy child with fine, curly blond hair, the youngest of the three children of George and Emilia Beider. George, an outgoing, clean-shaven man with broad shoulders and deep-set eyes, had served in World War I as the veterinarian of a cavalry regiment. After the armistice, he returned to his small village just south of Munich. There he began a prosperous career as a wagonsmith and veterinarian, making threshers and wagons for local farmers and tending to their animals.

Once a week, George would drive into Munich to buy iron bars, rakes, and implements for his plows from the warehouse owned by two Orthodox Jews. The fact that George had joined the Nazi party in 1933 did not sour relations between them.

In 1935, the Reichstag enacted the Nuremberg Laws denationalizing Germany's Jews and restricting them from most professions. George quit the party in disgust. He was not the kind of man to ponder the implications of Nazi racism, nor was he a politician. George simply knew in his heart when an injustice was being done, and he tried in his small, courageous way to ameliorate it.

From time to time, a car filled with Jews and the few possessions they could carry would pull into the Shell gas station next to George's workshop, which was run by his wife. Emilia, in addition to pumping gas, would make up packages of food for these refugees. On at least one occasion the refugees offered one of their family possessions in gratitude. George lamented the fact that such good people had been forced to run and leave everything behind.

In 1936, when Emily was eight, she began accompanying her father on his weekly business trips to Munich. While George attended to his other errands around town, he left Emily with the two black-frocked Jews, who never failed to indulge little Emily with all the ice cream she wanted.

A few days after one such visit, Emily, her older sisters Maria and Amilie, and George were leaving their home for school when Emily heard someone sneezing in the root cellar. Emily peeked into the dark cellar. Down below, she spotted one of her friends from the warehouse, ill from the cold. George heard his daughter, full of concern, asking the man if he was all right, and came running. He shut the door quickly, anxious that none of his employees discover that he was hiding Jews.

George was aware that the school officials encouraged children to inform on their parents. On the way to school that morning, he took his young daughter by the hand and said in a gentle but firm voice, "We're not going to talk about that, are we, Emily." By the next day, the sick old man had vanished.

George taught his children to read the Nazi newspapers with a critical eye. Even young Emily learned to tell fact from propaganda.

That July, George died unexpectedly. Emilia was told that her husband, only forty-seven, had suffered a fatal heart attack while playing a game of cards at the local club. For weeks after George's death, his good friend the village police chief tried unsuccessfully to convince Emilia to agree to exhume George's body in order to perform an autopsy. Soon thereafter, the chief died in similar circumstances. Although they had no proof, Emily and her sisters always believed that both men had been killed by the Nazis.

Like many German families, Emilia and her three girls suffered under the Third Reich. Emilia fell ill after her husband's death, and during the course of the war, she suffered two heart attacks. Emily, like many teenage girls, was conscripted by the state to work one hour before and four hours after school. She was posted to a bakery one mile away from the high school she attended in Munich.

Every day, she handed out bread to the *Ostworkers*, hundreds of whom shuffled through the long lines, waiting for their daily starvation ration. These were slave laborers—mostly Jews, Czechs, and Poles—who were worked to their deaths in an armaments factory less than a mile away from the bakery.

For three years, Emily worked on the women's line. Unlike the men, with their gaunt, withered frames, the enslaved women, yellow with jaundice, had become so bloated by hunger that they looked as if they would soon explode.

One after another, they would step to the front of the line and hand Emily a few pennies under the watchful eyes of the baker's wife, who played the concertos of Wagner, Mozart, and Beethoven on her piano as the starving ranks of prisoners shuffled by. Emily often broke the rule forbidding eye contact with these prisoners. She would search for some hint of recognition in their dead eyes. After ringing up their coins in the register, she would cut each prisoner a slice of bread. Emily would often try to cut an extra half-inch of bread for the pregnant women, but the baker usually caught her and hit her with a stick for her temerity.

Emily was often warned about her conduct, but such prohibitions served as an inducement and a challenge. Every evening, she would lie awake, sick over the hundreds of men and women who lined up before her every day.

In December 1944, the British dropped leaflets over Munich, announcing that a "Christmas surprise" would soon be coming. Emily had fond memories of prewar Christmas celebrations; in 1944, all she could look forward to was an ersatz coffee made from burned carrots. It was clear to Emily and her friends that the Reich had been defeated. She hoped that the surprise the Allies were preparing was an end to the war, an end to the senseless misery and suffering.

On Christmas Eve, they heard the drone of RAF planes and watched with delight as phosphorus flares on parachutes lit up the sky. "It's like a Christmas tree," Emily recalled one of the girls saying. "Maybe they will drop apples and oranges," unobtainable luxuries in war-torn Germany.

Instead of fruit, the British dropped incendiaries.

During the Christmas firebombing of Munich, Emily watched as many around her burned to death or drowned trying to extinguish their flaming clothes in the river. The bakery was destroyed, as was her school. Distraught, Emily deserted Munich and returned to her village. There she found her sister Amilie, who had abandoned her job in Berlin as an engineer in the Messerschmitt factory, now under Russian control; Maria; and her sickly mother.

One day in March 1945, two SD men in black uniforms with green piping arrived at their door. For the girls, it was almost like the devil himself had come calling. Amilie and Maria stepped outside to talk to them, while Emily strained to listen from an upstairs window. After fifteen or twenty minutes, Maria came running through the front door.

"Emily," Maria whispered breathlessly, "stop what you're doing. Climb out the window. They've come for you!"

Emily couldn't believe that the baker had reported her escape from the burned bakery or that the Nazis, even as their war machine crumbled, had nothing better to do than look for her.

Emily jumped out of a back window and made for the hayloft of a nearby farm while Amilie tried to convince the soldiers not to arrest her sister. She told them that the BBC was forecasting an imminent American breakthrough.

"The Americans are already in Pforzheim and Stuttgart," Amilie told the SD. The U.S. Army would be in the village within hours, and anyone caught in an SD uniform would be hung from the nearest tree.

The two men argued the merits of duty and desertion. One favored the former while the other wanted to head for the safety of the mountains near the border town of Passau. They could be halfway to Vienna before the petrol ran out, he argued. Amilie offered them each a set of civilian clothes if they would leave her sister alone. The war was over in any case. Better to look after yourselves, she counseled. The SD men took her advice.

The Americans did not actually arrive until many weeks later. They were received by the burgomaster, who claimed

38

responsibility for the proper burial of the two American flyers who had crashed in town in 1942. It was quickly revealed, however, that it had been Emilia who had courageously arranged for the bodies to be buried in the cemetery after the burgomaster had ordered them interred in the common criminals' area in fifty-five-gallon oil drums. Each August 15 during the war, Emilia had planted fresh flowers by the crosses of the two young Americans.

The victorious U.S. Army rewarded her mettle. Amilie was hired as a secretary for an American judge working at the Munich denazification trials. Emily remained jobless and passed her time attending the trials. As far as she could determine, the hearings were a farce. Two-year sentences were summarily handed out to former soldiers of the Reich—simple men caught in political show trials who were all but denied any defense.

"What are you doing in my court every day?" demanded the judge when Emily came to his forbidding chambers on an errand for Amilie.

Emily explained that she had nothing else to do. The judge laughed and said he had never seen anyone that young interested in such matters. He learned that she had been tutored in English and offered to find her a job.

In 1948, Emily received her security clearance and began working as a low-level clerk in the espionage and terror operation run by General Reinhard Gehlen, the former Nazi commander of Foreign Armies East. Gehlen was an invaluable American asset in the cold war. He controlled an organization of five thousand agents and was anxious to serve a new master. Washington wanted to roll back communism; Gehlen sold his spies and *provocateurs* behind the iron curtain to President Truman.

The newly formed CIA had given Gehlen a limited mandate, ordering him to restrict his activities to the collection and analysis of information. He was also forbidden to employ either Nazi war criminals or former SS men as agents. Gehlen, however, had many masters in the burgeoning American espionage bureaucracy. The State Department's Office of Policy Coordination (OPC), the innocuous-sounding title for State's in-house spy operation, gave the ex–German officer carte blanche in his efforts to organize guerrilla operations against the Soviets and their Eastern European proxies.

Each day, Emily was given a stack of British, West German, and East German newspapers and told to look for specific advertisements. It was in this manner that many of Gehlen's V-men communicated with their boss. When she found the advertisements, she cut them out and put them in an envelope that was picked up at the end of each day.

Emily worked in the Munich office for almost a year before she was offered a second job at the special-intelligence base at Pullach.

Pullach was a pleasant Bavarian town near Munich. On its outskirts, the Nazis had built a compound, surrounded by a ten-foot-high cement wall, for former top officials in the SS. Even former Nazi party leader Martin Bormann once made his home inside the Pullach complex.

Under Gehlen's leadership, Pullach became the secret cold war recruiting base for Nazi war criminals with expertise in covert warfare against the Russians. Gehlen's Nazis, now employed by the State Department, ran the anticommunist underground in Eastern Europe from Bormann's old villa. Not even the CIA, headquartered across the street in Rudolf Hess's mansion, knew the scope of what Gehlen and State had organized at the most protected espionage base in postwar Germany.

Emily, now a handsome woman of twenty-one, wore a short, Bergmanesque coiffure; her comeliness attracted her superiors. In addition to her duties in Munich, she became the hostess at a small private dining room reserved for Gehlen's American bosses. She was never permitted to walk unaccompanied within the compound or to fraternize with the Germans who worked for Gehlen. But Emily was naturally curious about Gehlen's operation, with which she had become somewhat familiar while working in Munich. On Saturdays, when business at the dining room was slow, she would snoop around the grounds on her own in hopes of discovering more about Gehlen's supersecret organization.

It was on one of these Saturdays that Emily first met John McIntyre. A devout Irish Catholic from South Boston, McIntyre looked like anything but a spy. He was a tough, streetwise kid from a tough part of town, but he wore the thick, horn-rimmed glasses of an accountant and had the reassuring unpretentious air of a bank employee. His eyes twinkled and his smile was warm and genuine.

John was a music major in his third year at Boston University when he was recruited by the army's Counterintelligence Corps in 1948. He was sent to the army's elite specialist course for covert agents at Fort Holabird in Maryland. There, at the only school of its kind in the United States, he had learned the ABCs of covert operations—gathering information, cross-border operations, and surreptitious entry. To test their skills, recruits were ordered to break into banks in Baltimore and Philadelphia.

In 1949, only the army could provide U.S. agents with such training. The CIA was in its infancy and borrowed Holabird alumni like McIntyre for its own covert operations.

After graduation, McIntyre was posted to Germany. He thought that the army had seconded him to a CIA base in Stuttgart. Instead, two Germans met him on the train from Frankfurt to Munich, and told him he was to stay on the train until it reached Munich.

McIntyre started to argue when one of the Germans pulled back his coat, revealing a pistol. McIntyre just smiled and said, "I never argue with a .45." John had joined the CIC because he loved adventure. It looked like he wouldn't be disappointed.

From Munich, McIntyre was driven by limousine to the compound at Pullach. He didn't know what to make of the armed German guards on patrol with their German shepherds in what was supposed to be an American facility.

It was a Saturday, and there was no one around to brief him about his assignment. He walked over to Bormann's former house and passed by an office where Emily sat struggling with a crossword puzzle. John suggested "Puccini" as one of the answers, and they struck up an innocent conversation. John asked where he could attend Mass. Emily gave him directions to a local church, where she saw him occasionally. But it would be six months before John and Emily began to date.

They were an unlikely pair. Emily was a striking blonde, but her wide, sad eyes at first glance appeared totally drained of humor. McIntyre could make her laugh, but Emily's war experiences still haunted her. She resented that the Americans had created a Shangri-la at Pullach for their Nazi enemies, while the good people of Germany were starving outside Pullach's gates.

John, in contrast, was a typical easygoing, backslapping American. He now knew all about the devil's bargain the United States had made with Gehlen and others like him, but he reasoned that America had a new enemy that these former Nazis could help defeat.

John had little patience with Emily's enduring bitterness at America's rehabilitation of the Nazis. "The war is over!" he would shout when they argued about his role in the enterprise. "You're eating well. You're fighting another war, Emily. We're too small for that. Enjoy what you have for the moment you have it."

Crusades were not John McIntyre's affair. He was a professional spy who loved his country and who had pledged to risk his life in order to free the captive nations suffering under communist oppression. He had been posted to Pullach as a covert-warfare specialist. It was soon clear that he was getting into a dirty business; to survive, he had to maintain a professional's detachment.

John played the game very well indeed. He was one of the handful of Americans who actually practiced the trade glamorized by James Bond. He bribed his way past communist border guards with cigarettes and bottles of liquor in order to rescue scientists or "sleepers" in Czechoslovakia, East Germany, and Yugoslavia whose cover had been blown or to make drops of money and information to the agents who remained. John used to tell Emily that his best friend was not the false passport he had been told to use on such occasions—and which he left with her—but Johnny Walker and Jack Daniels.

McIntyre ferried Nazi war criminals through Austria to Trieste, where they joined the infamous ratline to South America. He also took part in the debriefing of enemy agents at safe houses maintained by Gehlen along Germany's eastern border. These locations were known as "lemon factories," where captured spies were "squeezed" for information.

McIntyre made daring weapons shipments to the anticommunist resistance in Poland and led covert landings along the Baltic coast in speedboats filled with weapons. In the event of World War III, the reasoning went, U.S.-armed guerrilla fighters in Estonia, Latvia, and Lithuania could harass the Red Army from the rear.

On one such mission, John was aboard a rubber boat ferrying arms to the Baltic shore when a flare went off on the beach and machine guns trained their fire on the landing party. Many of his fellow agents were massacred as the powerful incoming tide pushed them helplessly onto the shore.

Pullach was riddled with informers and double agents who were not uncovered until the sixties. The British liaison officer back in Washington was the Soviet mole Kim Philby, who had organized the disaster that night on the Baltic shore. Heinz Felfe, the number-two Nazi at the base, was also a Soviet agent. While he worked for the Americans, Felfe gave the KGB the numbers of all the passports issued to agents like John. John had the good sense to make his way across borders with a bottle of booze rather than the compromised identity documents; most of his buddies weren't as cautious. They didn't survive their error.

John's decision to break all the rules enabled him to survive in this swamp of duplicity and treachery. He won the confidence of the most senior American officials managing the covert program. He became the unofficial adjutant to General Lucian Truscott, who had been sent from Washington to arbitrate the turf battles between the CIA and the OPC. Aside from keeping the general sober, John attended top-secret briefings where he learned the details of the dirtiest elements of America's secret war against the Soviets. He was present for briefings of contingency plans for a joint American-British military follow-up to Operation Barbarossa, Gehlen's failed invasion of the Soviet Union, during the war. He learned of the unofficial American program to assassinate pro-Soviet Ukrainian officials, and was hospitalized after a training accident with a prussic acid gas gun.

Emily, as a result of her Saturday strolls, was preparing her own personal file on Pullach. Her father had not died to see Americans feting Nazis, no matter how useful they were. She was young and, she believed, invincible. She would single-handedly document, expose, and end the collaboration between Germany's tormentors and its American saviors.

McIntyre was furious when, in late 1951, he discovered Emily's freelance investigating; he was also terribly concerned. A young woman who had befriended Emily at Pullach had just been exposed as an East German spy. The Americans turned her over to German intelligence. John had later been told that she had committed suicide. John warned Emily that a similar fate awaited her if she was discovered.

There was only one way to stop her. Soon after this encounter, John and Emily were married. In October 1952, their first son, John, was born. Emily had been willing to risk her own life to record Pullach's secrets, but she couldn't endanger the lives of her husband and child. She closed her files on Pullach.

For the next year, the McIntyre family traveled together, following a unique spymaster's itinerary. While John conducted business at safe houses throughout Germany, Austria, and Italy and made occasional dashes into the Eastern bloc through Trieste, Emily and the baby would stay in nearby hotels. Weekends were spent on long drives delivering care packages to John's accommodating friends, who guarded the Iron Curtain border.

McIntyre's career as a spy came to an abrupt end on Christmas Eve 1953. He arrived home and announced to Emily that they were leaving for the United States that very evening. John's identity had been revealed to the KGB, and Europe was no longer safe for him or his family. Emily had only enough time to pack a couple of suitcases. The U.S. embassy was opened that night to stamp a visa in Emily's German passport. Within hours, John and his young family were secreted aboard a troopship bound for the United States. No one other than McIntyre's immediate superiors, not even his or Emily's families, knew where they had gone.

The ship was filled with American GIs returning home. Other than Emily, there were only seven women—all WACs—on board. The winter crossing was rough, the weather blustery. The ship's passengers, most of whom were seasick throughout the voyage, never ventured onto the deck. Many never left their bunks. Little John, however, thrived during the voyage. While Emily was confined to her stateroom, John ate every meal at the captain's table, his highchair lashed to the table to prevent it from sliding across the room when the ship lurched in the high seas.

John and Emily moved in with John's family in Dorchester, Massachusetts. John was tired of leading the harried life of a spy and was fed up with safe houses, dirty tricks, and treachery. He found a profession that suited his newfound desire for monotonous security, becoming a salesman for a vending-machine company. He dabbled in local politics. As the years passed, old friends from Pullach would occasionally visit, entreating him to come out of retirement. The answer was always the same. "Name me one spy," John would say, "who ever lived long enough to watch his children grow up."

During their European trip in the summer of 1969, John, Emily, and their sons John and Chris and their daughter Patricia visited Emily's family and the old cold-war friends whom they had left so precipitously many years before. During the days spent in her ancestral village, Emily told her son John for the first time about his grandparents' defiance during the war. She even discovered that one of the gifts offered to her parents so long ago by fleeing Jews—a small copper-point picture—still hung in the family's business office.

Bad Reichenhall lies along the Austro-German border near Salzburg. At the end of a cable car that reaches to fourteen thousand feet stands a large villa with a grand veranda opening toward the mountains. John had once used the place as a safe house. While he was there debriefing agents, Emily, with their newborn son John, would stay in an equally idyllic small hotel in the town below.

The McIntyres returned to the town that summer. The innkeeper remembered John, who was so delighted to see the old woman that he waltzed her around the dining room. She was honored that he had returned with his family and refused payment for their nine-day visit.

Burden of Truth

John was fascinated by the reception awarded to his father in Bad Reichenhall and at the numerous other villages hugging the Iron Curtain that they visited that summer. Would he ever be able to match the courage that his father, mother, and grandparents had shown? he wondered.

The summer they spent in Europe, Emily would later recall, was the last time her son John was ever truly happy and at peace with himself. That autumn, John was driving a friend home from a school dance when they were broadsided by a speeding car. John suffered major internal injuries and a skull fracture when he was thrown through the windshield. As the doctors attended to him in the ICU, John was frantic with worry about his friend.

The doctors kept insisting that the boy was all right, but John didn't believe them. When told that his friend was in an adjoining room, John ripped out his intravenous tubes and staggered into the hall. Only then was he told the truth: his closest friend had died instantly in the crash.

John was in the hospital for months. Lawyers for the young woman who hit his car charged that John was responsible for the accident and threatened to file a civil suit against him for the negligent operation of a motor vehicle. The police had cleared John of any criminal wrongdoing; his blood-alcohol level was zero.

Although John recovered physically, he was permanently scarred by the emotional trauma of his friend's death, the draining months of his own recuperation, and the lingering, irrational belief that somehow he was responsible for the tragedy.

He pulled away from those he loved. Chris and John shared a bedroom. Chris, an adoring brother of ten, would often jump into his big brother's bed during the night. After the accident, however, Chris never did.

John withdrew into himself. He lost all trace of his former

boyish smile. It was as though the accident had stolen John's youthful joy and exuberance.

John's parents tried to shake him of the belief that he was responsible for his best friend's death. They pointed to Ted Kennedy's ordeal over his recent accident at Chappaquiddick. If Kennedy could recover, they suggested, so could he. John was not impressed by such comparisons. He was emotionally adrift, without a compass to guide him.

John's parents had a difficult time persuading him to finish his last months of high school. He had planned on an engineering career, but before the end of his first semester in the engineering program at Boston's Northeastern University, John dropped out. He walked into the kitchen one evening, sat down at the table where Emily and John were having dinner, and informed them of his decision to leave Northeastern and join the army.

Both parents were shocked. Never before had John even hinted at a desire to enlist—and now he was talking about volunteering for service as an infantryman in Vietnam. Emily tried to argue against such a decision, but John wouldn't hear of it. "Let's not talk about it," he said curtly. "I've made up my mind and that's that."

In the fall of 1970, John enlisted in the army. He may have hoped that the military would offer him what the ocean had offered in his youth—the challenging embrace of simplicity and purity. He may have thought that it would give a sense of structure and meaning to his life that the car accident had destroyed. Or he may have believed that, just as his father had found meaning and commitment in his service to his country a generation earlier, so would he.

Chris had another explanation for John's sudden determination to get to Vietnam. Ever since the car accident, Chris felt that John wished for death. He concluded that John had no fear of dying because he had no desire to live. At the time of John's enlistment in 1970, the U.S. Army was the perfect place for young men with death wishes. America's war with Vietnam still raged, and the fighting was grinding out its weekly toll of casualties.

In another war, in another army, John might have been one of those crazy heroes who win every battle with death until the last. This army, however, put the boys with the brains far away from the blood and guts of the battlefield. John's score on the army's intelligence test put him in the top one percent of recruits. The Army wanted him to forego the infantry, and serve with military intelligence instead. The idea appealed to John. As he saw it, intelligence was where the truly brave men served their country. John agreed and reported to the Army Security Agency's intelligence school at Fort Devens, about an hour's drive from Squantum.

John made the most of his opportunity. He excelled in the school's intelligence-operations program, just as his father had at Fort Holabird. John's expertise lay in leading-edge intelligence technologies. He learned the mechanics of state-of-the-art intelligence communication and security, the means by which top-secret messages are securely passed between the highest commands—and intercepted, as well. He mastered the high arts of decryption and decoding, accomplishments that put him among the top communications specialists in the country.

This was heady stuff for a young man not yet twenty who had dropped out of college. He took classes with seasoned officers, who resented John's proficiency. Their careers depended on their performance in the twelve-month course, and they did not take kindly to being upstaged by some whiz kid without stripes. John wasn't bothered by their envy. He was enjoying himself too much, rising to each challenge and reveling in the army's secure embrace.

Even a severe eye injury, caused by a beer bottle thrown in a bar one night, couldn't retard his progress. The camp commandant recognized that John was a diamond and bent the rules so that he could complete his course despite the time he missed during his recuperation.

John's final scores put him third in his class. The desire for self-destruction appeared to be in check. In a few short weeks, he intended to ship out, not for Vietnam, but for Germany—and not as a pack-toting grunt but as a first-class passenger on the fast train to the upper echelon of military intelligence.

Just when he seemed to be getting his life back on track, John's naiveté and misplaced sense of duty to a friend put his future in the army in jeopardy. John's friend Chuck was like a second brother to both John and Chris; John had even taken Chuck's SAT exams in high school. Despite the safety of John's assignment, Chuck feared that John would somehow get himself killed. Determined to keep his good friend out of harm's way, Chuck planted a small quantity of marijuana in John's army locker and then phoned in an anonymous tip to the military police that John was a drug dealer. Chuck later sobbed out a confession to John. He had never dreamed that John would be sent to jail for a first offense.

John never considered informing on his friend, nor did he even try to mount a defense. At the trial, John told the court that he knew how harmful drugs were to national security because his father had once worked in intelligence. But he lamely suggested that marijuana was probably less harmful than alcohol. He innocently thought that if he pleaded guilty and apologized, everything would be made right.

The judge wasn't at all impressed with his logic. As he saw it, John was on the threshold of a great career and had thrown it away for some pot.

John was court-martialed on July 28, 1971. The judge busted him to private from specialist E-3 and sentenced him to three months' hard labor in an Army prison in Rhode Island. From the time he was two years old, John hated any form of captivity. Some good advice could have saved John from such a vindictive punishment, but he was determined not even to inform his parents of his problems. Instead, he listened to his friends and foolishly refused to appeal.

John saw himself as a victim of those more powerful than he. His security clearance had been revoked, ending any hope of a career in military intelligence. As he sat in the stockade, John faced a future as an army grunt—cannon fodder for some vainglorious general. He was no longer prepared to play that role. Just weeks before the end of his sentence, he decided to run for it.

On August 9, 1971, the stockade guards came running to quell what sounded like a race riot at the back of the army prison. While they were busy in the rear, John calmly walked out the front gate and stepped into Chuck's waiting car.

John had no real plan beyond driving out to California. But he only made it as far as Colorado before the army caught up with him.

At the Fort Carson army base near Colorado Springs, John finally got a break. He was befriended by Captain Dick Sullivan, an army attorney from Southie only six or seven years older than John. He processed the court-martials of kids being sent home from Vietnam for drug convictions and interviewed them as they passed through Fort Carson.

Sullivan had seen kids convicted for heroin offenses who had not been treated as harshly as John had been for his first marijuana infraction. He took a liking to this intelligent, brash, wayward young man and kept him out of prison while he looked into his case. The two Irish boys from Boston became good friends.

John realized that he had at last found a supporter in the army bureaucracy, someone who was willing to give him the benefit of the doubt. When John explained the true circumstances of his case and raged against the extraordinarily severe punishment he had received, Sullivan promised to see what he could do. He kept John on as his typist while he moved the army bureaucracy into gear.

Sullivan arranged for John's case to be reviewed by a competent attorney. John's father, when told of his son's predicament, seconded the attorney's decision to file a formal appeal. A review of John's sentencing confirmed its undue harshness. John's conviction was overturned and expunged from his record. The army even reinstated his security clearance, a remarkable testament to the injustice of John's original conviction, and he was requalified as a top ASA graduate. A career in military intelligence opened before him once again. John's parents breathed a sigh of relief.

John was posted to NATO's Strategic Communications Command Center in Karlsruhe, West Germany. Because it served as the traffic cop for the top-security communications channels of the allied governments and eavesdropped on the high-level communications of the communist world, STRAT-COM was one of the most sensitive bases in Europe—the holiest of holies in state-of-the-art military communications.

At STRATCOM, John worked with the most advanced espionage technology, massaging computers for intelligence information. He became a specialist in Chinese-language decryption systems and real-time intelligence communication. He spent his days in front of a bank of computers, searching for ways to decipher coded Chinese messages even as they were being sent. He fancied himself a spy of sorts, like his father before him, only he was mastering high-tech methods his father couldn't have dreamed would exist.

John sat at the center of an international code-breaking and eavesdropping system from which no one, friend or foe, could hide. At that time, Secretary of State Henry Kissinger was secretly preparing the ground for President Nixon's historic visit to Mao's China. Kissinger, paranoid about leaks, piggybacked on the military's independent secret-communications network for much of the back-channel diplomacy in

Southeast Asia he conducted unbeknownst to officials at the State and Defense departments.

John learned more about such matters than he was prepared for. International diplomacy is a seamy, double-dealing world full of poseurs and hucksters. And the back channel is the sewer where the government secrets flow. The things this naive young man read off his computer screens made him sick.

Access to U.S. covert-operations files gave John an insider's look into the blood-soaked legacy Nixon and Kissinger were creating in Southeast Asia. John discovered that American oil companies, anxious to protect their tanker routes off the coast of Vietnam, were selling oil to Hanoi as well as Saigon. He learned from Chinese intercepts during 1972 that secret negotiations to end the war—Kissinger's back channel to Le Duc Tho sometimes routed through STRATCOM—were nothing more than an election-year ploy by the Nixon administration to keep the North Vietnamese at bay until after the November balloting.

The Phoenix assassination/pacification program had become a bloodbath under the direction of the Pentagon's Special Operations Group. Teams of Marine Reconnaissance Units, Navy SEALs, and Army Rangers under John Singlaub's command were dropped into Cambodia, Laos, Thailand, and North Vietnam to wreak havoc wherever they could. These soldiers were terrorists skilled in the arts of mayhem and assassination. Many of the men whom the army listed as missing in action were members of such squads, sent into combat without dog tags or U.S.-issue fatigues. They had been killed in this secret war, unknown to the American public, unauthorized by Congress.

John believed that he was engaged in a noble profession and that intelligence work and military service were ways that a man could serve his country with honor. He thought that he had found a place where he could fit in, a career in which he could be proud of his achievements. Instead, he discovered nothing but treachery and cold-blooded murder festering beneath the civilized niceties of manicured diplomats. John's inflated expectations and the ideal world he had created for himself were shattered by this confrontation with reality.

There were times when his father, after squeezing an enemy agent for information or returning from a run on the ratline, would sit in a safe house and drink himself into oblivion. But John senior had no illusions about how the world worked, and soon he was sober and ready for another operation.

The seventies were far different. Among young John's military contemporaries, navy yeoman Charles Radford copied documents routed through the back channel and leaked information to Congress and the press. Similar revelations by Christopher Boyce exposed CIA efforts to overthrow the Australian government and their successful campaign against Allende in Chile.

John wasn't driven to drink or do drugs by what he learned at STRATCOM. And he neither blew the whistle nor defected. Instead, John locked what he had learned inside himself. He spent every free hour off base visiting his Aunt Amilie and her husband Hanno. John's uncle was a former Wehrmacht spy chief, who had been blacklisted during the Cold War because he refused to work with Gehlen's thugs. The U.S. Army still maintained close ties to Gehlen's successor organization, the BND, the West German intelligence service. The BND still listed Gehlen's old lie that Hanno was a security suspect, and told STRATCOM that John was visiting a blacklisted German. For John, this false and vindictive attack on his uncle was the last straw. He wanted out of the army.

But John's intimate knowledge of its top-secret communications posed a problem for STRATCOM. It was expected that such specialists would never leave government service.

Their skills could only be utilized by the military services and the supersecret National Security Agency—or by a foreign government.

When it became clear that John's tenure would soon be over, the army asked John for permission to deprogram him—to use experimental drugs to wipe his memory clean of the military secrets he had learned. John's father advised his son to refuse such debilitating therapy. No one was going to fry his son's brain, not even the U.S. government.

The army began the chemical deprogramming anyway. Despite the effects of sodium pentathol, John escaped from the hospital and called his relatives. The army relented. John was given an honorable discharge and awarded a disability benefit ostensibly because of his lingering eye injury, but actually to cover up the damage caused by the attempted brainwashing. As long as he lived, John never trusted anyone in government again.

3

~~~~~~

A NEW BEGINNING

After his discharge, John returned to Squantum and found a job as a lifeguard on Cape Cod. For weeks on end, he sat on the beach staring aimlessly at the ocean.

In the fall of 1974, John gave Northeastern another try. Again, he dropped out after a month. Soon after, he started driving a cab. While waiting for a fare one afternoon at Logan Airport, John bumped into Chuck, his old friend from high school. Chuck was also a cabbie, but he was better known as the guy who had emptied Quincy Bay of all its stripers.

Chuck was a fish thief. And he taught John, who had never fished as a kid, his nocturnal trade. John and Chuck often engaged in some late-night illegal clam digging. A hard night's work would bring them a catch worth one hundred dollars. They wore flashlights attached to headbands as they raked the mud flats along the tidewater.

One night, the two friends were discovered by gun-toting officers from the Massachusetts Department of Natural Resources. The rules governing maritime theft gave the lawmen, or the fisherman whose livelihood was threatened by poachers, a ready opportunity to shoot first and ask questions later.

"Stop or we'll shoot," one of the officers yelled to the boys.

John ordered Chuck to run for it. A bullet whizzed over their heads. Chuck froze and raised his hands in surrender.

"You idiot!" screamed John, who never considered leaving his friend alone to face the angry cops. "They don't shoot people for clam digging."

The officers weren't playing games. One of them pointed a gun at John's head. John held up his hands in mock surrender.

"Shoot me, officer," John deadpanned. "I've got an unregistered .45-caliber clam in my shirt pocket."

John and Chuck were let off with a warning, not for the first time, and certainly not for the last.

Pollution had drawn incredible schools of fish to the sewer outlets between the Hull peninsula and Deer Island. It was illegal to use a net to drag for these fish, but at fifty cents per pound, John could clear seven hundred dollars on a good night.

Late one evening, the *Grey Ghost*, a fifteen-foot trihull powered by a 135-horsepower Evinrude, raced out of Squantum. Despite the full moon, the speedboat, running without lights, was nearly invisible. John, now fishing on his own, had painted his fish-poaching skiff navy-camouflage gray from stem to stern.

When John reached the fishing grounds, he whispered a query into his two-way radio.

"Anything?" he said.

The sudden crackle of John's voice startled Chuck, perched atop Squaw Rock. From this vantage point above the Squantum shore, Chuck had a clear view from the gut of Thompson Island off Squantum, where John had set his nets, north to Boston.

"Nothing," Chuck responded absently. He reached into the pocket of his windbreaker for a bottle and took a sip of cheap whiskey to ward off the chill that rose from the water. The liquor was a good companion. After a few more swigs,

A New Beginning

Chuck nestled against the rocky ledge. Instead of eyeing the harbor for police boats, Chuck dozed.

While Chuck slept, the *Jesse*, a sixty-foot patrol boat carrying twelve hundred horsepower, closed in on the unsuspecting *Grey Ghost*. Fumbling in the dark, the *Jesse*'s crew fought to remove the stiff canvas that covered the .50-caliber cannon on the foredeck. They opened the ammunition boxes, fed in a belt of bullets, and pulled the bolt back to lock in the first round.

John heard the distinctive rumble of the *Jesse*'s engines while she was still on the harbor side of Thompson Island. He quickly cut his nets loose just as the *Jesse* thundered around the island's north end. John spun his wheel, just in time to see a couple of smaller police boats racing across the shallow gut at the island's southern shore. John's only hope of evading the trap was to turn southwest and head for the bridge between Long Island and Moon Island. If he made it under the bridge first, he might be able to lose his pursuers.

Once he had passed under the bridge, John swung the *Grey Ghost* hard to port and raced eastward along the darkened coast of Long Island. As he rounded the island's northern end, he turned hard to port again on a circular course that would bring him back to where he first spotted the *Jesse*.

But instead of continuing parallel to the shore, John headed the *Grey Ghost* directly toward the water's edge. Straight ahead lay the tangled, rotting pilings of a long-abandoned pier. John ran at full throttle toward a gap in the pilings only a few inches wider than his boat. He screamed through the opening, slammed the throttle into full reverse, and came to a dead stop under the wreckage of the decrepit wharf.

From his blind, John watched the *Jesse* shoot around the island and past the pier. John waved a mocking good-bye and settled back with a smile against the gunnels, patting the rail where he had patched up the bullet holes from a previous chase. Despite the interruption, John still had close to a full-night's catch on board.

The *Grey Ghost* pulled onto the beach where Chuck was waiting with John's truck. There wasn't any time for John to be angry. The fish were quickly off-loaded into boxes and packed onto the open truck bed. It was still dark when John drove the truck away from the beach and made for the Quincy on-ramp and Boston's wholesale fish market.

For hours, a team of agents from the Massachusetts Department of Natural Resources had been cruising both sides of the expressway in search of a small truck entering from one of the Quincy interchanges. The *Jesse* had lost the *Grey Ghost*, but the police knew that such a small operator would have to sell his catch that day.

Agent Cumo spotted John's truck as it pulled onto the lightly trafficked Southeast Expressway. Blue lights blazing, he closed in for an arrest. As Cumo's car pulled alongside John's truck, he rolled down his window and bellowed an order to pull over. John just grinned and waved. If he could make it to the next exit, he'd be able to lose Cumo in the warren of Quincy's familiar back streets.

Cumo did not want to give him that chance. He leaned out of his window and banged his nightstick against John's truck. John swerved his wheel sharply left and then right, expertly smashing the right front fender of Cumo's car. Cumo's driver blanched and backed off, conceding John a solid lead as he screamed onto the off-ramp curve.

Waiting at the bottom of the ramp, his car completely blocking the road, was an off-duty Quincy cop who had followed Cumo's pursuit on the radio.

John slammed to a stop, got out of the truck, and smiled at the cop, whose pistol was pointed right at John's nose. Cumo's car screeched alongside. The driver rushed out of the car and began punching John furiously for smashing his fender. John didn't fight back. He knew he had it coming to him. He was already in enough trouble and could well do without the additional problem of an assault charge.

"What the hell's going on?" bellowed the cop as Cumo pulled his driver off of John. "What's he got in there? Heroin?"

"No," yelled Cumo triumphantly, "fish."

"Counsel for the defendant?" intoned the clerk of the Quincy district court, showing only the slightest indication of interest.

No one replied. The audience in the courtroom started at this novel intrusion. Not only was the attorney absent, John himself had yet to appear.

After a few moments of confused silence, John, grinning, walked through the main entrance and made his way quietly to the table reserved for defendants.

"Present, Your Honor," he said.

John calmly surveyed the staring faces that filled the courtroom. He was dressed in ragtag fisherman's gear, complete with bait bucket, rod and reel, and grimy trousers reeking of stale fish. John's face, in contrast to his attire, was scrubbed clean. He had shaved off his full black beard. His dirty blond hair was nicely combed today. He looked like a good boy down on his luck.

That's exactly what John wanted the judge to think. He apologized for his appearance but explained that all of his other clothes were on the truck that had been seized by Cumo. He couldn't afford a lawyer or even bait for his lobster pots, because Cumo had also seized his commercial fishing gear along with the fish in his truck.

"Your Honor," John began contritely, "I admit I was out there that night fishing. I didn't think that there was anything illegal about that."

"Your Honor," interrupted Cumo, "the defendant is

charged with illegal use of a gill net. Every fisherman knows that is illegal."

John looked puzzled.

"Net? What net? I don't use a net. Did you find a net anywhere on my boat or in my truck?" asked John simply.

Cumo was suddenly speechless.

"Well, where's the net?" queried the judge, sensing a quick dismissal.

"Your Honor," stumbled Cumo, "we don't have to have the net. This is absurd. He had over one thousand pounds of fish on his boat."

"How'd you catch the fish?" asked the judge, turning to John.

John explained the feeding frenzy that regularly took place by the sewage outflow between Moon and Thompson islands. Any skilled fisherman could haul in as many fish as he did in the course of one night.

The judge was smitten. He began discussing the fine points of fishing with the well-spoken defendant. When they were through chatting, the judge dismissed the case and ordered John's property returned.

As they walked out of the courtroom, Cumo congratulated John for talking himself out of a certain conviction.

"I had to do something," John said almost apologetically. "I can't believe I got off either."

Even though John maintained a genuinely friendly familiarity with Cumo and the judge, he hated the power and authority they represented. His court-martial and the shattering experience at STRATCOM only reinforced the distrust and fear that followed in the wake of his friend's death—distrust of the guardians of right and wrong, fear of losing control over his life to them.

Since he was seventeen, John had maintained a safe-deposit box. He had never applied for a credit card, preferring to use his father's instead. Like his spymaster father, John

A New Beginning

knew how not to be a number. And like his father, he knew how to break all the rules, thumb his nose at the system, and survive. A few nights after his courtroom antics, John was back in the poaching business.

The ocean had always been like a cradle. He loved its solitude and its clarity; life on the mainland contained too many ambiguities. When John was on the water, he could forget, in the challenge of the wind and the salty spray, the drift that had overtaken his life. No matter how bad the weather, John found security and courage in the knowledge that the rules governing the contest between him and the elements were immutable.

On the fourth of July 1975, John came home to announce that he was moving in with Robbi Ronan. Robbi was a leggy, attractive blonde a couple of years younger than John. Robbi lacked the discipline and interest to attend college, but she had proven herself to be an energetic and imaginative employee at a local company and had been promoted to a responsible management position. She and John had met at a bar and had dated for less than a year before moving in together. John was about to end a brief and unsuccessful marriage. Robbi's high-spirited playfulness brought out feelings John thought he had buried. They had fun together, dancing until the early morning hours or heading out at a moment's notice for a rowdy weekend on Cape Cod. But while John was emotional, sentimental, and committed, Robbi was a schemer, always looking for an easy way to make a buck.

In many ways Robbi was John's link with the world. It was through her that he bought all of his legal guns. All of his bank accounts were in her name. Only the *Grey Ghost* and the *Night Stalker*, a thirty-two-footer used for legitimate lobstering, were legally owned by him.

Soon after taking up with Robbi, John decided to take some of his poaching profits and build his own lobster boat. Since his release from the army, John had taught a boat-building class at the University of Rhode Island. He was a real craftsman and enjoyed introducing others to this dying art. He had no intention of quitting his lucrative late-night enterprise, however, at least not right away. John planned to construct the lobster boat himself and, over the next few years, slowly build up a legitimate stake as a lobsterman. After his disastrous marriage, a good woman and a steady job might put his life on an even keel once again.

His relationship with Robbi, though, was rocky from the start. Within six months, the roller-coaster pattern of argument, breakup, and reconciliation was established. John lived apart from Robbi, at his parents' home and later in his own apartment, more often than he lived with her. Robbi had been another expression of his faith, and it bothered John that he was failing again to make a lasting commitment to something, or someone, beyond himself.

John made better progress with the boat he first christened the *Robbi Ronan*. He got a permit from the city of Quincy to cut a few of the many oak trees growing at the city's dump. He and Chris felled the trees, loaded them on a flatbed, and trucked them to a mill in Rhode Island. The finished wood was transported to the university workshop for seasoning and construction. While he was building the boat from the seasoned oak, he worked in the driveway next to his parents' two-story white colonial, making more than two hundred lobster pots; Robbi knitted their green conical nets.

The finished boat was a trim white lapstraked twenty-four-footer with a wide beam that sloped upward toward the bow. John built a small deck house to protect the control panel and shield him from wind and surf. On either side of the boat, he installed the winches that would draw the pots up from the ocean floor. After things with Robbi soured, he renamed the boat the *Royal Scam*, after his favorite song. The crashing rock music matched the fiery lyrics about ancient warriors who fought bravely and went to Valhalla.

A New Beginning

John was at a Squantum dock working on the *Royal Scam* one day in 1979 when he was approached by someone he would have taken for a cop if it were not for his heavy foreign accent.

"I'd like to talk to you," the man said directly. He was tired from a sleepless twelve-hour plane trip, and his back was hurting. Now he was catching the full force of the New England spring chill, with only a skinny blue windbreaker for protection.

"What about?" John asked, not at all sure what to make of this stranger.

"I'd like to charter your boat," replied the man unconvincingly. John noticed that he was carrying a decidedly unnautical briefcase.

"I'll pay you well for one hour. I just want to talk to you. It'll be worth your while," he said bluntly, handing John a hundred-dollar bill.

John helped his well-paying passenger into the *Royal Scam* and started the engine.

When they had gone a few hundred yards offshore, the foreigner told John to drop anchor so that they could talk. The chop quickly proved too much for him. John sensed the man's discomfort and suggested that they move to a beach on one of the uninhabited islands that dot Boston Harbor.

When he stepped onto shore, the man's face betrayed such obvious relief that John had to smile. The man smiled too and had a good chuckle at himself.

Together, they climbed atop some nearby rocks and watched the freighters make their way down President's Road, the main harbor channel, to the tugs that would steer them into a safe berth.

The man introduced himself as an employee of Israel's scientific mission to the United States. His job, he explained, was to identify and recruit consultants with skills of interest to Israeli universities. "We want to hire you as a consultant to design a graduate course on advanced telecommunications equipment," he said. "I'm prepared to offer you an annual retainer of fifty thousand dollars."

John said that he had the wrong man.

The Israeli pulled a copy of John's military record out of the briefcase. "Perhaps we have made a mistake," he said, feigning regret. "We wanted to interview John Leo McIntyre, Jr., Social Security number 021-42-3214, born October 8, 1952, formerly specialist E-3, assigned to Company C, Third Battalion training regiment, United States Army Security Agency. According to these records, a person of that name has considerable experience with certain telecommunications equipment. You are the same John McIntyre?"

John nodded, somewhat surprised.

"According to these records, you were hospitalized during training for a severe eye injury. Yet you not only managed to complete the ASA course, you graduated near the top of your class. Not surprising in view of your aptitude scores," he noted almost absentmindedly as he thumbed through the file. "You had a great career ahead of you in the military.

"Although it is not in your records," he continued, "we know that your specialty at STRATCOM headquarters involved Chinese-language decryption systems and real-time intelligence communications. You were one of the best in the world. Why did you quit?"

"You seem to already know everything about me," John said coolly. "You tell me."

Out of the briefcase came a green cardboard folder with the words "Summarized record of trial by court-martial."

"You were framed, no?" suggested the man kindly. "But you pled guilty and waived your right to counsel. Were you protecting someone?"

John nodded again, annoyed that a stranger should know so much about him.

The Israeli had not once mentioned an intelligence con-

A New Beginning

nection, but John knew no one else in Israel could be interested in the expertise gained at STRATCOM. He wasn't fooled for a second.

"Let's cut the crap," John said calmly. "You are no more a scientist than I am. You are a recruiter for Israeli technical intelligence. Your COMINT [communications intelligence] and SIGINT [signal intelligence] facilities are more than adequate against the Arabs. Their signal security is a joke and you know it. My skills are way too advanced.

"There is only one way you could use my expertise," he added. "Why do you want to spy on America?"

The Israeli spook let a few minutes pass in silence while he gathered his thoughts. The kid was smart, there was no question about that. It would be best if he told him the truth.

The agent admitted that he was indeed an intelligence agent. Israeli intelligence, he explained, had recently discovered that the United States was withholding from Jerusalem vital information about Arab military capabilities and intentions. Even worse, Israel's military secrets were being passed on by officials anxious to curry favor with U.S. client states in the Arab world. He gave the *Liberty* incident as an example.

A few years before John arrived at STRATCOM, Israeli intelligence discovered that the U.S.S. *Liberty* was stationed offshore to monitor secret battle orders and leak them to the Arabs via the British. The Israeli cabinet sent a courier to ask for volunteers to stop the *Liberty*'s codebreaking in order to protect an imminent Israeli counterattack. Half the Israeli squadron refused to shoot at a ship flying the American flag; the remaining pilots had to attack several times until all the *Liberty*'s antennas were destroyed. Senior American officials, caught in the act of betrayal, asked the Israelis to pretend that the raid was an accident, and quietly reimbursed Israel for compensation paid to the wounded Americans on the *Liberty*.

Israel had to know the quantity and type of information the Americans were still transmitting to their Arab friends.

67

That's where John came in. The skills he learned at STRAT-COM could be employed to intercept and decipher U.S. data and intelligence transmissions to Israel's Arab enemies. "We picked you because we thought you might understand and help us," finished the Israeli.

"Why me?" asked John, genuinely perplexed.

The Israeli was ready with an answer. He pulled the last folder from his briefcase—the trump card that had catapulted this young American with no previous ties to Israel to the top of his list of potential recruits. This time, John couldn't read the cover of the folder. It was in Hebrew.

"Because of who you are," the stranger replied as he glanced at his open notes. "Because of the way your family raised you. Your last name is Irish. But you were born in Germany, as was your mother and grandfather. Your grandfather enlisted in the Nazi party in 1933."

"You bastard," said John. "If you think you can blackmail me into working for you because of my grandfather, you've got the wrong guy."

The Israeli wiped his glasses. He was weary after his long flight, but he couldn't allow himself the luxury of fatigue—or anger.

"I am not a bastard," he replied with a steel calm, "and neither was your grandfather. Quite the opposite. Your grandfather was one of the heroic Germans who tried to stop Hitler before it was too late. Didn't you know? Didn't your mother tell you what your family did for our people?" He asked whether his mother ever told him about the Nazi war criminals hiding out in Pullach, the kind of men who may have murdered his grandfather.

"How did you know my mother was at Pullach?" asked John.

"We read her file as well," came the reply. "There were Jews in Pullach too. It was before my time, but I understand your Mr. Rockefeller promised that if the Zionists kept their

68

mouths shut about Pullach, he would see to it that every nation in South America either voted in favor of the creation of the state of Israel or abstained. It was a devil's bargain for these Jews, but what could they do? They were forced to choose between justice and a nation. They chose Israel and kept silent about Pullach.

"Sometimes we Jews do not have a choice," said the Israeli. "You do. Think about it. You are the third generation of a family that has taken great risks to help others. It is your heritage, your fate. We need you. Talk it over with your family if you wish."

It was a good pitch, but John wasn't buying. He told the agent no.

He was suspicious of the agent's entreaties. He discussed with his father the possibility that the U.S. Army was testing his loyalty. John senior agreed that John had probably been approached as part of an ASA security sting.

Whatever the source of the offer, John wasn't interested in spying for anyone. He wanted nothing to do with someone else's secret wars. And no one who knew him or his family would think that a McIntyre would betray his own country for a few pieces of silver.

Not long after his encounter with the Israeli, John moved to an apartment in Chelsea, just north of Boston. Chelsea is a depressing, tired town, a seedy, unrehabilitated cauldron of ethnic politics squatting unceremoniously beneath the Mystic River Bridge, which connects Boston with the prosperous suburbs along the North Shore.

This gritty working-class community across the river from Charlestown's Bunker Hill never recovered from a fire that leveled a large part of the city in the mid-seventies. After that, anyone who could left for the suburbs. Chelsea boasts two main attractions: a restaurant featuring singing waiters and a ramshackle steam bath in a white concrete building squeezed between triple-deckers, where cigar-chomping businessmen and assorted shady characters come for an afternoon sweat.

Oil-laden ships destined for Boston's refineries have fouled the city's pride as well as its shoreline. Everything, and everyone, in Chelsea has its price. For a time, there was hope that a gentrified Main Street would restore the city's lost propriety, but the new trees and scrubbed brick facades just look like rouge on a whore.

John, searching for a cheap dock near his apartment where he could keep the *Royal Scam* and store and repair his lobster pots, took a ride up Chelsea Creek. This narrow, foul tributary of the Mystic River divides east Boston from Chelsea. Tankers loaded with their cargo pass from polluted Boston Harbor into the oily waterway, where tugs tow them to the petroleum storage tanks lining the mammoth piers. The area is littered with old wooden barges, rotting piers, and industrial debris rusted from age and exposure; it's held hostage to the constant din of jets landing at nearby Logan Airport.

Walton's Pier, at 107 Marginal Street, Chelsea, is one of countless similar places along the creek. On the inland side of Marginal Street are the hulks of once-proud captain's houses—now stuffed with immigrants from Asia and Latin America—whose Federal pillars are neglected, whose clapboards are cracking, and whose once-fine views are blocked by refinery tanks and huge mounds of road salt hoarded for the winter behind barbed-wire fences.

From the water, Walton's looks as though it's being squeezed between the giant silver fuel-storage tanks on its left and the bricked-up warehouses on its right. Its main pier sits about one hundred yards from each of Walton's inhospitable neighbors and juts out a good fifty yards into the grimy creek. Remnants of a bygone era—like the *Pilgrim*, a once-grand schooner now imprisoned by the muck, old pilings, masts, and timbers—are everywhere, carelessly abandoned for the water to claim.

A New Beginning

John stepped off of the *Royal Scam* onto Walton's Pier. He didn't have much money to put out for docking privileges, but from the look of the place, Walton was in no position to be greedy.

Jim Walton was addicted to industrial auctions. Scattered over his lot was a collection of tractor-trailers, cargo containers, wooden boxes, sewer pipes, and slurry machines, bargains that Walton couldn't afford to pass up but seemed to have no earthly use for. A two-story warehouse, which doubled as the corporate headquarters of Walton Industries, was set in the middle of his property. There was a workshop on the first floor; Walton's offices, decorated with old nautical tools and ropes, occupied the upper floor.

Jim Walton was Welsh, a bit of a bully who liked to stare people down until they looked away. His wages were low, and he worked his people so hard that turnover and equipment breakdowns seemed to keep his operations in constant chaos. His main business was cleaning up toxic waste. Walton was perfect for Chelsea.

Walton also ran a marine-salvage business and leased heavy equipment. Local gossip said that Walton's Pier was used occasionally as an off-loading dock for small marijuana shipments of ten or fifteen tons that the odd lobster boat would ferry from the mother ship to tractor-trailer trucks waiting in Walton's yard. Walton himself claimed he had no stake in the drug business. If anything, he was strictly on the fringes of the Mafia drug syndicate, no different than any number of dock owners who were paid handsomely to make their piers available and to keep their mouths shut.

"What the hell do you want?" snarled Walton as John walked into his office.

"Are you Mr. Walton?" asked John with deliberate courtesy. Walton was put off guard by this simple expression of respect. John did not blink at Walton's staring, and quietly stared right back.

71

"You're all right, kid," he responded. "Whadaya want?"

John explained that he was looking for a place to rebuild his lobster boat and had noticed from the water that Walton seemed to have plenty of available space.

Walton questioned John about the repairs he wanted to make, who would do them, and how long it would take. It wouldn't be the first time the Drug Enforcement Agency tried to plant a narc on the waterfront. Walton wanted to make sure he knew who he was dealing with.

John's answers impressed him. It was obvious that he knew about boats. Walton judged that John might be useful to have around.

He offered John a cheap mooring for the *Royal Scam* and even volunteered the free use of his crane to lift the boat out of the water for repairs. But Walton explained that John would have to find his own float to attach to the pier. That night, John donned a wet suit and, with help from a pair of bolt cutters, "liberated" a floating dock in South Boston and ferried it to Walton's Pier. Larceny was a skill Walton appreciated. Sooner or later, he might need John's talents himself.

During the rest of 1979, John did nothing but catch lobster and pursue some after-hours poaching. Walton's was just a parking place for the *Royal Scam*.

In 1980, Walton won a big contract for asbestos removal. Very few companies had been licensed and certified by the state government, and Walton Industries stood to make a lot of money in a seller's market. Walton was quick enough to know he needed someone smart and personable to run the crews. He had watched John repair the *Royal Scam* and had on occasion hired him to fix the odd crane or salvage barge. John had proved himself a talented, hardworking craftsman who got the job done—rare gifts among the half-baked characters who dominated the docks.

In early 1980, Walton offered John a full-time job as a foreman in the asbestos business. John jumped at the chance

A New Beginning

but insisted he be paid off the books, in cash. Walton, never one to argue with a request made on the wrong side of the law, readily agreed.

John had good reason to believe his life was at last beginning to take on a steady, predictable rhythm. He had a solid, well-paying job, and Walton gave him the authority to run his operation without interference. The business was profitable. Rumor was that more than one tractor had dumped a load of the hazardous waste into Chelsea Creek. It wasn't STRAT-COM by a long shot, but at Walton's, John found that he was putting his life in order.

John felt so good about Walton's that he brought his brother Chris into the operation.

Chris was barely into his twenties, taller and huskier than his older brother. Like John, his hair was blond and cut short, but his face, with its naturally well-proportioned features, was always clean-shaven, whereas John usually wore a beard to make himself look older. Despite his size and strength, Chris spoke softly and smiled easily. He was a good kid, as ready as the next for a fight but never one to pull the illegal pranks and cons in which John always found such pleasure. The demons that had chased his brother never pursued Chris. He loved his older brother in the undemanding, admiring way younger siblings often do.

Chris deferred to John naturally and completely, accepting John's authority without dissent. When they fought, Chris invariably lost, although he was bigger and stronger. Neither brother was particularly verbal. Like their parents, they bore their grudges stoically. Heart-to-heart talks were inconsistent with their self-images as tough, rugged men.

Chris quickly advanced to foreman of Walton's asbestos crew. For a kid so young, he was doing quite well. In a good week, he could take home up to two thousand dollars. But unlike John, Chris didn't mind paying taxes.

After work, John, Chris, and the rest of Walton's crew

would hang out at Heller's, a workingman's bar down the street from Dillon's steam bath. They'd have a few beers, swap stories, get loaded, and find release in an occasional fight before making their way home.

Heller's, a two-story corner brick building, faces a back-street Chelsea intersection not far from Walton's. A Schlitz lantern hangs over the entry. At first glance, it seems just another nondescript seedy bar, but toward the back is a cashier's cage. Mike, fiftyish, stocky and gray, was owner, bartender, and cashier. He wore a fifteen-thousand-dollar Rolex that everyone called "The Texan" because of the two long gold horns on either side of its face. For a small fee, Mike cashed the checks of the local workers, some of them illegal aliens who didn't like anything that smelled official. Others like Chris would get off work too late to cash a paycheck at the bank. No one who valued his health ever passed a bad check with Mike.

To guard against robbery on Fridays, when $1 million could change hands, legend had it that Mike would post two men with shotguns in the second-floor windows overlooking the street. A kid once tried to rob Heller's, not knowing what went on there. Marveling at his good fortune, he walked out with two garbage bags full of cash. He supposedly made it to the middle of the street before the guards opened fire. Mike ran out, grabbed the cash, and brought it inside. The police found a dead body in the street.

4

~~~~~~

SECRET SOLDIER

John seemed to have found his niche in the predictable, tawdry life along the Boston waterfront. He kept the *Royal Scam* for occasional lobstering. But John's illegal poaching gave way to lazy evening sails around Boston Harbor in the *Hudson*, an old red tug belonging to Walton, with Chris and friends.

"We got a little problem," said Walton to John one day after he had returned from a day on the water. Walton had bought a bankrupt fleet of six fishing boats, the *Eleanor Eileen* trawlers. He expected some trouble claiming them, he explained, so he wanted John to arm himself and organize a crew to bring the fleet from their mooring in East Boston over to Chelsea.

Although John and Chris didn't realize it, the six vessels were owned by a friend of drug importer Frankie LePere, who planned to use the trawlers to smuggle bales of marijuana into Walton's at night.

John, Chris, and some of Walton's men had no trouble repossessing the trawler fleet and bringing it to Walton's that night. But the McIntyre brothers knew fishing boats when they saw them, and it was obvious that these southern trawlers wouldn't survive their first nor'easter offshore. Chris examined the hydraulic-fluid levels on the huge winches used to pull in the trawler's fishing nets. They were empty, and they had been for some time. All the gears were rusting from disuse.

"Whoever owned these boats before didn't use them for fishing," said Chris. John agreed and commanded Chris to keep his eyes open and his mouth shut.

Walton had John strip the fleet of electronic gear—equipment necessary for fishermen but a dangerous convenience for a drug boat vulnerable to electronic eavesdropping. In the weeks and months that followed, Chris spent a fair amount of time repairing the fleet, which kept appearing with bows and sideplates smashed from offloading operations at sea.

John had heard for quite some time about the marijuana smuggling going on at the pier. Although he worked days and the smuggling invariably took place at night, John quickly suspected the reason for the empty tractor-trailer trucks and the sealed containers on the pier.

From the first, he wondered about who was behind the operation. They had to have a lot of money. He heard that a lumper—the crew member who carried the heavy bales of marijuana—received ten or fifteen thousand dollars cash for an evening's work.

John never told Walton about his suspicions about the *Eleanor Eileens* or the countless other indications of the drug trade being conducted. Walton was a cautious fellow. John realized that his best hope for keeping his job lay in biding his time, and winning Walton's trust and confidence.

Joe Murray was patient too. Unlike the Israeli spy, who made his pitch and disappeared, Murray brought John along slowly, patiently awaiting the time when he could approach him. He was always looking for new talent. Joe was well known around the grimy nooks of Chelsea and nearby Charlestown, where he owned the Celtic Pub next to the Teamsters local. Only a handful of insiders knew this genial

Irish pub owner was a rising star in the Mafia smuggling racket.

Until the early eighties, New England was merely a backwater for drug smuggling. Florida, owned by the crime organizations, was where the real action was. The Mafia turned the coast from Saint Augustine to Miami into a network of cocaine caches and marijuana ports. There were so many errant bales of marijuana floating ashore that fishermen in Key West called them brown grouper.

The profits generated by drugs dwarfed the sums earned from all of the old rackets put together. At one time, nearly a third of all the currency in America was on deposit in Florida. This stash of drug cash fueled the extravagant lifestyles of a new generation of mobsters. Pressure was on the government agencies to stop the flow of drugs into the state.

Florida was eventually bottled up by federal agents. Drug freighters making their way up from Colombia were met by a phalanx of federal and state drug hunters, who, working in concert for the first time in a generation, managed to implement effective and innovative drug interdiction strategies. The FBI, Coast Guard, DEA, and U. S. attorneys were winning the war against drugs in the Sunshine State. Millions of dollars in confiscated cash and property was distributed to underfinanced local and state police units fighting the drug wars.

When Florida got too hot, the Mafia dons simply moved their operations north to New England, ideal because of its existing crime infrastructure and its jagged coast dotted with secluded bays and inlets perfect for smuggling. The government, a much slower animal than the Mob, was still pouring its antidrug resources into Florida. The New England–bound freighters, however, sailed right on by.

This change was good news for Joe Murray. By 1980, he was thinking of taking over the defunct LePere network and building it up from a nickel and dime smuggling group into the region's largest drug operation, off-loading drug-stuffed freighters, ferrying the contraband ashore, and transporting it in tractor-trailers and railroad cars to distributors as far away as Chicago. On the Boston waterfront, Murray simply duplicated the blown Saint Augustine operation. He even used the same boats—the *Eleanor Eileens*, a fleet of beamy Gulf trawlers purchased from Frankie LePere—which were tied up at Walton's between jobs.

Despite the tiny cargo capacity of the *Eleanor Eileens*, pot smuggling made Joe Murray a rich man. By the beginning of 1981 the IRS figured that Murray was taking home, and not reporting, hundreds of thousands of dollars annually. He paid cash—hard to trace (but easy to remember) tens and twenties—for everything from a thirty-foot pleasure boat, a Mercedes, and a truck to a lakefront home in Maine. In the spring of 1981, Murray decided to expand the marijuana smuggling dramatically until he could buy into the far more lucrative cocaine, hard drug, and counterfeit currency rackets. Without Dublin's knowledge, Murray planned to exploit his local Provo contacts to do so.

The local IRA had access to U. S. government officials with a soft heart for Ireland who could be counted upon not to be around when a marijuana shipment arrived, as long as it was generous Joe, who gave so much to the cause. Murray, in turn, impressed the Mafia with his mysterious ability to bring in large quantities of marijuana unmolested. Joe hoped neither the IRA nor the Mafia would ever learn how he was managing a dangerous double game for his own profit.

Murray's exploitation of his IRA links wasn't entirely mercenary. He had grown up on the fringes of IRA politics in Charlestown. Even as far back as 1890, the Boston Irish had been smuggling guns to their republican brothers in Eire. During World War II, Boston was a key center for guns, money, and soldiers in the battle for Irish independence. When independence was won after the war, the IRA withered.

Secret Soldier

For decades afterward, the old leadership of the Boston IRA—traditional Catholic politicians in the mainstream of Democratic party politics—rested on the victorious establishment of the Irish Republic. At most, it sent a few guns over to the boys.

In the seventies, the Provos—the Provisional Irish Republican Army—were established in Ireland under the leadership of an Army Council to inaugurate a more militant opposition to the sudden arrival of British troops in the Northern counties who often sided with radical Protestant groups. The Provos wanted to defend Catholic neighborhoods from organized mob violence. To make this strategy work, the IRA required larger quantities of guns; unfortunately, most of them were intercepted by the British before they got close to the Irish shore. New York was then the center for pro-IRA smuggling, both of cash and of weapons. The U. S. Customs Service was kelly green, and the IRA sympathizers infiltrated the longshoreman's union as well. This network of customs officers and union officials working for the IRA came to be known as the Emerald Society.

When this New York connection was shut down by zealous prosecution of the Emerald Society, Murray saw an opportunity to make both Boston and himself indispensable, to use his IRA infrastructure and Mafia-controlled port and feather his own nest in the process. Murray, who during the early seventies had done little more than pass the hat in the Celtic, now promised the IRA that he could smuggle money and guns out of Boston. And he assured the Mafia leadership, which had just lost Florida, the LePere organization, and Assistant U. S. Attorney Twomey, LePere's important mole in the government, that he could bring large quantities of drugs into Boston without risk.

By the late seventies, Murray had become a leader in the Boston IRA, sending crumbs to the northern counties, including occasional weapons, and giving refuge to Provos on the run. The old IRA leadership in Boston turned a blind eye to what Murray told them was his peripheral involvement in the drug trade in return for a share—little did they realize how small a share—in the marijuana profits. It was easy to rationalize selling pot to college kids as a harmless way to raise money for the cause.

Murray was always looking for good, trustworthy men, Irishmen like himself, to join his drug operation. Walton had told him about John, highlighting his reliability and discretion. Kids from Belfast who wre working on the pier seconded Walton's good words. John was worth pursuing. Murray decided that the time had come to check out this young man for himself.

John had just returned from a job cutting underwater pilings at a nearby pier. "Someone wants to meet you," shouted Walton to John as he stepped onto the dock.

John followed Walton over to his houseboat.

Walton had built his Chelsea home atop an early nineteenth-century barge. There were several of these tied up at his pier, including one enormous hulk which in an earlier incarnation had served as a chicken coop. Walton's barge was considerably more comfortable. The floating home boasted three bedrooms, an enormous kitchen, a living room, and a pilothouse on the second floor. One of Walton's favorite pastimes was shooting rats with his .38 as they peeked into the kitchen from the pipe holes in the floor.

"This is Joe Murray, a friend of mine," said Walton.

Walton had no friends in the accepted meaning of the word, and Joe Murray didn't trust Walton nearly enough to admit him into his small circle of intimates. After assuming LePere's operation, Joe kept Walton at arm's length, paying enough attention only to keep Walton from asking too many questions about Joe's nighttime use of his pier. Walton preferred to know nothing of Murray's activities, but had been asked to keep an eye on John. New faces were always suspicious to Murray.

When John was introduced, Murray's smile made John feel as though he had just met an old friend. Joe quickly discovered that he and John had a lot in common. Both were military men; Joe was a member of a National Guard unit that trained with the Green Berets at Fort Devens. He shared John's fascination with guns and fast boats and enjoyed nothing better than a little hunting and fishing. John's father had run unsuccessfully to be the state representative from Quincy, and Joe never forgot the name of an Irish politician.

Joe could see that despite his intelligence, John was just a regular guy, most comfortable in jeans and a T-shirt, with a beer in his hand. Murray himself drove around in a used Mercedes and lived in a simple two-family house; he appreciated John's unaffected simplicity. Like Murray, John preferred people who knew the value of a dollar. In fact, he kept track of every nickel. Even as a kid he preferred to make gifts for his family, a chess set or a ship's model rather than waste money on store-bought gifts. He and Murray seemed much alike.

As they sat on Walton's houseboat that day, Murray asked John about his family, his politics, and his knowledge of the struggle between Catholics and the Protestant majority in Northern Ireland.

John had no politics to speak of and told Murray that he knew and cared little about Ireland. "You should," Joe replied. He asked John to come to the Celtic Pub one day after work. He had an Irish friend he wanted John to meet.

The Celtic Pub occupied the ground floor of a triple-decker building right next door to the Teamsters local and directly opposite the Sullivan Square off-ramp of Interstate 93. Its heavy wooden entry door was flanked by windows protected by grilles of wrought-iron shamrocks.

The Celtic attracted an eclectic clientele. Loan sharks wearing six-hundred-dollar suits and packing a piece mingled with soot-covered laborers from the nearby Boston Edison power-generating plant, Teamsters coming in for a beer after work, and office workers from the Schraff's candy factory.

The IRA crowd hung out at the far end of the bar, near the dart board—and the rear exit. Some were Black Irish—thin, with black hair and olive skin—the descendants of the Portuguese who immigrated to Ireland in the fifteenth century. These men were all fugitives from Ireland who had come over to work in Boston, getting paid under the table. Once in Boston, Murray would take them into his protection. They'd work for him as gofers, lumpers, or collectors for a couple of years before returning home. It was a tough crowd to associate with. Later on, John warned Chris that these young men would "just as soon kill you as look at you."

Murray's friend was one of these outlaws—a seventeen-year-old IRA soldier. John would not have picked the black-haired man for an Irishman were it not for his heavy brogue. That night at the Celtic Pub, he told John his melancholy tale about growing up in Northern Ireland, about how he buried his father, a fallen soldier in the IRA, and vowed to continue the fight.

John felt an intimate kinship with this anonymous dark-haired boy—a kinship not of faith and vengeance but of loss, personal suffering, and the search for commitment. He felt an intimate, sincere identification with the suffering people of Ireland, represented so tragically by his new friend. Here was a young man who had found a just cause worth fighting and dying for.

"What do you want from me?" John asked Murray, who had been sitting nearby. "What do you really want?"

Murray simply shrugged his shoulders. He told John he was responsible for smuggling young men in trouble with the British, like the one sharing a beer with them, and pointed out the importance of knowing one's heritage.

Joe had learned from Walton about John's expertise in

military communications; he in turn told the Provos during one of his frequent trips to Ireland. The IRA was in sore need of someone with John's talents. High-tech British counterintelligence was crippling the IRA. It had lost more arms shipments than it cared to remember because British agents had successfully bugged the vessels, which were then seized when they entered British or Irish waters. The IRA needed a counterforce that could stymie British efforts and intercept and read British communications. John could be their answer.

After John left the bar that evening, Murray asked the young fugitive about his impression of the STRATCOM veteran.

"He's either a gift from heaven or a plant," the boy replied.

During the next few months, Murray kept a close but indirect eye on John. A steady stream of young men with Irish brogues appeared for work on Walton's asbestos crews. None ever stayed for long. John befriended these Irishmen. The America he took for granted appeared in a different light when seen through their eyes. They marveled at the city of Boston and knew much about American history. John, in contrast, began to realize how little he knew of his Irish heritage.

From his young friends, John heard the partisan's side of the organization and learned of Britain's oppression of the Catholic minority. They were amused by his often naive questions about their native land. Were the IRA terrorists? he wanted to know.

Certainly not, they replied. It was the British, with their hit teams based in Lisburn, Northern Ireland, who were the true instigators of terror.

After work, they'd all head for the Celtic Pub. There the expatriates making temporary accommodation in Charlestown and Cambridge would swap stories about home. As the evenings would progress and the dark pints of Guinness would begin to work their magic, John and his Irish buddies would become crooning comrades in the liberation of Ulster.

"Here's to Ireland undivided, to all good Irishmen and true. . . . Up the rebels." John listened to the bar patrons roaring out these words about a dimly understood battle halfway around the world. The enthusiasm of the working-class sons of Irish immigrants was picked up by manicured patrons from Admiral's Hill, a gentrified island of Charlestown. John would join the Irish immigrants when they laughed at these armchair Irish patriots. In doing so, he separated himself, and what he was prepared to do for the cause, from them as well.

The IRA was then enjoying an unprecedented amount of American media attention and public sympathy. Several Provos had been imprisoned by the British. The men were treated like common criminals; the Provos insisted they were POWs, captured in their battle against the British. The imprisoned Provos began a hunger strike to the death to have their POW status restored. They won the support and attention of Americans, who watched with morbid curiosity as the British steeled themselves against capitulation. One after another, the Provos starved themselves to death.

John contrasted the selfless commitment of Provo prisoners like Bobby Sands with that of the barroom warriors he knew at the Celtic and bristled at the comparison. He began reading about the country from which his great-grandfather had emigrated and its endless struggle against the British. The trouble in Ireland easily became a battle between good and evil. Ulster was just another country the British had stolen and did not want to give back. Heroes like Bobby Sands were fighting and dying while he and the rest of Boston's fair-weather champions of Irish freedom were doing nothing for their homeland.

The Irish newcomers at Walton's and the Celtic were contemptuous of their assimilated American brothers, and they encouraged John's newfound enthusiastic militancy. The British, they told him, would never leave Ireland unless they were forced out. Violence in defense of justice, counseled these true believers, was no vice.

John was won over. He envied the IRA fugitives who had the commitment to something larger than themselves that he lacked. He thought about his German grandfather who had risked his own safety and that of his family by heroically standing up for Jews in Hitler's Germany. He recalled how his grandmother had defied the local Nazis and buried the two American soldiers. And never far from his thoughts were the exploits of his parents, their keen sense of right and wrong, and their determination to act on their convictions. How could he not follow in their proud footsteps by becoming a soldier in the war to free his Irish countrymen?

Was there anything John could do for the IRA? he wondered aloud. Word of John's interest quickly found its way to Joe Murray, who, in his own time, would have a ready answer to John's question.

John showed up as usual at Walton's one cold November morning at half-past five, about a half-hour before Chris and the rest of the asbestos crew were due to arrive. He went down to the pier to get something from the *Hudson*, and he saw the tug's foredeck littered with marijuana from a bale that had smashed open during the previous evening's drug shipment. The stupid lumpers had simply missed the grass in the darkness. It was stupid carelessness. John was shoveling the grass into a trash can when he saw Chris heading toward him.

"Get out of here," John yelled. "Don't come down here."

Chris dutifully turned around and headed for Walton's workshop and a cup of coffee.

There weren't enough bags in which to stuff the grass, so John carefully swept the marijuana into a pile and spread a tarpaulin over it. Then he headed straight for Walton's office. He'd been around Walton's long enough to know how the smuggling was conducted. Chris and he had even stolen a look at an off-loading operation one night. The smugglers were so certain that the Chelsea police wouldn't bother them that they never bothered to block the view from the street outside the fenced-in compound.

"You aren't paying me enough to risk getting involved in this shit," he said flatly to Walton as he threw a bag of pot across Walton's desk.

Shocked, Walton agreed that he wasn't being paid to get involved with the marijuana either and denied that the grass belonged to him.

"Why don't you ask your buddy, Mr. Murray?" Walton suggested. Murray, he continued, was the man behind the *Eleanor Eileen* drug trawlers and the *Hudson* as well. Walton, knowing how enthusiastic John was about the IRA and his budding friendship with Murray, told him that Joe was probably sending all the proceeds from the smuggling operation to the fighting Irish.

Walton's scam worked. John had never suspected that Murray was involved in the smuggling, but the fact that he was made the adventure even more attractive. So too did the news that the drug profits were going to the IRA. Just like the young soldiers had told him, violence in the defense of justice was no vice. John walked out of Walton's office, more slowly than he had entered, and went back to work. He would not blow the whistle on Murray.

In early December 1981, soon after his conversation with Walton, Murray offered John a job as a lumper on the *Eleanor Eileens*. The pay was fifteen thousand for one night's work carrying bales of grass from the boats to the trucks. Murray was ready to take a chance with him. If it turned out John was a plant, he'd catch a bullet in his head and find a watery grave. It wouldn't be the first time it had happened.

Secret Soldier

During the few weeks that he worked as a lumper, John proved to be an intelligent, reliable, and discreet member of Murray's smuggling organization. He did what he was told and even had some suggestions for increasing the security of the operation. Joe and John were spending more time together—fishing, at the Celtic, and at Joe's house, with his wife. They'd admire each other's guns and talk about Ireland.

Toward the end of December, 1981, Murray decided to make his move. John would be thirty next year, and it was time to think about the future. If he was going to be involved with the IRA's drug shipments, Murray counseled, he might as well make a real, lasting commitment. And why not make it to the Provos? Was he interested in joining the IRA? Joe warned John that such a decision couldn't be taken lightly. Once John was in, there was no turning back. He would have to accept a soldier's discipline, taking orders as well as giving them. And just as in any other army, if John disobeyed, he could be court-martialed and even executed.

Even if John did want to enlist, Joe continued with a salesman's flair, he might not be accepted. Some of the IRA members at the Celtic and the Provos working at Walton's still harbored suspicions that John, because of his army-intelligence background, might be an undercover informer.

John voiced concerns of his own. He feared for the security of the drugs-for-guns pipeline to the IRA as long as some of the people from Walton's were involved. From what John had seen over the last two years at the pier, some of the lumpers had trouble organizing coffee breaks, let alone a drug-smuggling operation. One night, they might not have enough trucks to haul the night's catch away, so they'd let it sit in a trailer with the door wide open. John voiced other concerns about the security of the smuggling operation.

John tried to impress upon Murray that some of the lumpers working at Walton's Pier were thugs and drug users who would sell their own mothers if it would benefit them.

The lumpers were sloppy, careless, and stupid. Joe, John insisted, would be foolish to trust them or even Walton.

Murray just laughed. John was taking a real chance bad-mouthing one of Joe's agents. Joe told him not to worry about Walton, he didn't know anything and didn't want to know. The lumpers were mercenaries to be sure, Murray explained, but they were *his* mercenaries. The crew of misfits were merely hired hands. They moved drugs for money, not for the IRA. Greed would keep them quiet.

John wondered aloud how Murray's drug boats managed to keep out of the clutches of the Coast Guard. As far as he could determine, they were a disaster waiting to happen. It was not unusual, for example, to see one of the *Eleanor Eileen* trawlers, bales of marijuana stacked under a tarp on deck, making its way at night right through Boston Harbor. John knew from his poaching days that the Coast Guard was a determined, competent outfit. Sooner or later they'd catch on.

Murray laughed again. "You don't have to worry about that," he said. "*We* are the government. The IRA has informants in places you wouldn't believe."

John realized that unlike his interview with the Israeli agent, where he was in control, Joe was drawing him into the drug pipeline on Joe's own terms, and it frightened him. Murray would never reveal such details if he didn't feel that he could trust, or intimidate, John. John had heard that dead bodies sometimes turned up in the back alley of Murray's pub. Chelsea creek was also known as a graveyard for the incautious. And John knew that he too could be targeted for execution if he refused Joe's "offer" to enlist in the IRA.

These high stakes made the enterprise even more appealing. In any case, Joe was right. It had been ten years since the bitter disappointment at STRATCOM. Although he'd really enjoyed the last couple of years, John had to admit that he was just treading water. It was time, John decided, to have the courage of his convictions.

On an icy night in January 1982, John ran the engine room on one of the *Eleanor Eileen* trawlers as she made her way out of Chelsea Creek and down through President's Road to the mouth of Boston Harbor. Past Boston Light, the swells rose to six feet on a line. A small freighter, bobbing in the waves, was waiting for them.

John had been promoted by Murray from lumper to supply officer—a signal of the IRA's readiness to accept John as a member. His job was to transport fuel, food, and other provisions to the mother ship for her return journey, wherever it might take her. Instead of a lumper's wages, John would be paid twenty-five thousand dollars each time he made a run.

That night, the two ships ran up against each other as the trawler drew alongside the mother ship. Her cranes spilled bale after bale of marijuana onto the *Eleanor Eileen*'s bouncing deck as the ships continued to bash each other. John watched this deadly comedy from a hatch below. He knew the peril posed by two boats as large as these in such close proximity in anything but a becalmed sea. If it wasn't so dangerous, the Keystone Kop antics on deck would be funny. There had to be a safer, more efficient way to get the job done. John knew he could easily find such a way.

In February 1982, John was inducted into the Provisional wing of the IRA in a secret ceremony attended by the small cadre of the Boston IRA. John pledged his allegiance to the Provisional IRA constitution, promised to bear arms in the cause of a united Ireland and vowed to fight in her defense and for her freedom. He had taken a similar oath before, when he had joined the U. S. Army, but now he was a secret soldier in a war of his own choosing, a war in which, like his father before him, his role would go unheralded. John was proud of himself for making this commitment and flattered to be the youngest of the Boston Irish Provos.

After the January drug run, John decided that if the IRA was going to profit from the drug trade they might as well do it efficiently. If Murray could arrange to keep the Coast Guard out of the way, and evidence pointed to the fact that he could, then John promised he could reorganize the logistics of the entire operation and bump the thugs on Walton's pier out of the way in the process.

First to go were the *Eleanor Eileen* trawlers. They were too unstable a platform for off-loading the marijuana from the freighters. They could transport only fifteen or twenty tons each, far less than the capacity of the bulging mother ships anchored offshore. The more trawlers required to service each freighter, the greater the risk of engine failure and a beached trawler full of grass.

Frankie LePere had originated the idea of using the *Eleanor Eileen* fleet to ferry marijuana into Boston. He figured that if he spread out the marijuana shipment among a few small ships, they could scatter more easily in the event of a Coast Guard sting. Murray's source in the Coast Guard, however, removed the danger of a bust at sea.

John discarded this entire system and replaced it with one of his own. Walton owned a giant steel barge—the *D108*, which was built to ferry tanks and armored vehicles across the stormy English Channel during World War II. It had even participated in the invasion of Normandy. Like everything else Walton owned, the *D108*, used for marine salvage, was old and worn from exposure. The platform itself was a good ten feet above the waterline. Its thwarts were dotted with old truck tires hung as bumpers over the rusted and water-stained sides. This 150-foot long, 40-foot wide mammoth floating dock could haul tons of marijuana per trip if she was outfitted correctly.

John installed one of Walton's small yellow-cabbed cranes on the deck and welded it in place near the stern. Then he cut eight huge deck hatches into the barge's watertight compartments.

The *Hudson* was enlisted to tow the *D108* to its late-night rendezvous. Because of its massive steel hull, the barge could slam all night against a freighter without any danger of either being damaged or sinking. Its huge deck offered an easy off-loading target for the freighter's cargo cranes. Pallets full of marijuana bales could be dropped from the freighter anywhere on the deck. The crane on the *D108* would move them into place, and the crew would cover them with black plastic tarps. This system, unlike its predecessor, was safe, fast, and productive. The *Eleanor Eileens* could be retired, and the number of lumpers, engineers, and pilots—all of them capable of squealing to the Feds—reduced.

John's reorganization did not stop at the water's edge. The main danger of detection was not at sea but at the unloading dock. Automation was the key to improving the efficiency of this end of the operation. First, however, some security had to be established. John ordered the sinking of a couple of old barges at Walton's Pier. The *D108* would be moored behind them, out of view from the street. He also covered Walton's perimeter fence with beige sheathing as an additional obstacle against snoopy observers. Next, John set to work on the new off-loading system itself. He gutted the interior of the burnt-out chicken-coop barge and ordered a bed of industrial rollers installed. These rollers consisted of heavy sets of rails with countless small wheels between them, similar to the rolling tracks that supermarkets use to slide boxes of groceries.

John wanted to apply the supermarket principle to bales of marijuana. The *D108*, hidden from view, was moored right next to the chicken barge. The heavy bales slid down a set of rollers and disappeared into the old chicken coop. Once inside, the bales would make a right turn along the roller path and exit into a tractor-trailer. Gravity did all the work, and the bales could be loaded into waiting tractor-trailer trucks as fast as the crew could tip them off the *D108*. The trucks, usually five or six for each shipment, were loaded in one-third the time and with far less manpower.

John masterminded the new system, but Clayton Smith perfected it. The off-loading system in the chicken coop was all his idea.

Clayton Smith was a transplanted Irishman who had left Belfast for the United States after the war. Despite the fact that he emigrated when he was already well into adulthood, Clayton spoke in a perfect down-East accent. When he talked, his head bounced as if it were a real effort to push the words out. Clayton always wore a blue and white engineer's cap, but if he was feeling particularly spry, he'd exchange it for a psychedelic hat. He was almost seventy and had lost muscle tone, but he nevertheless put in a full day's work repairing Walton's machinery with men half his age.

Clayton was a very quiet and engaging companion. His age separated him from the rest of Walton's young crew; he drank bourbon at Heller's while they drank beer. But, perhaps because of his age and experience, he became a sounding board for John, and he was always ready to listen to whatever anyone wanted to tell him. John and the other young men at Walton's found themselves wanting to talk to him, almost as they would their fathers. When John first discovered the pier's involvement in the smuggling trade, he went to Clayton for an explanation. Clayton, it turned out, knew all about the *Eleanor Eileens* and the *Hudson*, including the old Saint Augustine operation.

This ancient mariner was the only one at Walton's who had offshore experience. He was a former merchant marine and a sea captain, as familiar with heavy diesel engines as most men are with their wives. He began working for Walton in the fall of 1981, repairing the *Hudson*'s antique engine. Clayton was adept at coaxing ship engines back to life and enjoyed teaching John what he knew. Together, they rebuilt

Secret Soldier

the tug's engine from the bottom up. The pilothouse was ripped off the deck, and Chris was sent in to scrape down the engine's cylinder walls, a job he likened to cleaning a six-foot-long garbage can from the inside.

Clayton and his wife had a home in Cherryfield, Maine, but they lived instead on Walton's houseboat, which Walton had vacated after moving to an estate in Boxford. The crusty old-timer was therefore one of the only employees around during both Walton's legal day shift and Murray's drug-filled night shift. Clayton couldn't help but know about the marijuana trade, which went on just outside his bedroom window. He was paid well to keep his mouth shut.

By the spring of 1982, John and Clayton were fast friends, and the *Hudson* and the *D108* were actively engaged in the marijuana trade. Once a month, Murray arranged for a shipment with someone called Mr. Big in Saint Augustine. The rendezvous off Boston Light between the mother ship and the *D108* was planned for a time and place where Murray's source told him that the Coast Guard would not be patrolling that night.

John thought Murray shipped the pot to Chicago, so as not to arouse local suspicions. But from Walton's, the marijuana was actually transported to warehouses throughout the Boston area, including one in South Boston owned by Joe and run by his brother Mike. Joe labeled every bale so he could keep track of distribution and income. Part of the shipment was immediately sent by truck or rail to locations outside New England. Joe wanted to get rid of most of the marijuana before it started hitting the streets of Massachusetts—and before the DEA began looking for the source.

After a while greed took over and Joe handled distribution in the Boston area. He worked with people like Joe Bangs, a former police officer.

Bangs and his partner would arrive at a prearranged meeting place with a couple of trucks. They would give the keys to Murray, who, together with another driver, would then drive to a warehouse and load the marijuana. Each truck would haul at least seventy-five bales. Joe had marked each bale with a number, beginning with 101. Then Joe would return the trucks to the two men, who drove to roadside stops in Medford and Dorchester or to Bangs' house in Tewksbury, where each bale was weighed and marked. Within a few days, after Bangs distributed the pot and collected some money, Joe would see partial payment as paper-bagged packages containing $100,000—in ten-, twenty-, and hundred-dollar bills—were delivered to his home. Joe kept the bags in a kitchen cabinet over the stove; he was always paid in full before Bangs saw his share of the profits.

Each shipment aboard the *D108* could bring in more than three hundred bales of marijuana weighing between fifty and a hundred pounds each. The street value of marijuana was between fifty and one hundred dollars per ounce. With a straight face, Murray claimed that "Mr. Big," the Mafia importer, and the retail distributors made most of the profits, leaving only a few hundred thousand for the IRA war chest every time the *D108* was pressed into service.

But Murray was secretly acting as importer as well as distributor. Even after paying off the IRA, the lumpers, and the truck rentals, one of Joe's partners told the Feds, "Murray was netting over $1 million on every load that he did with them and [he] gave them a piece of the action on about 20 loads between 1981 and 1983." The Provos had no idea how rich they were making Murray.

During 1982 and 1983, John worked exclusively for Murray and stockpiled what seemed to him to be a lot of cash. But money was only one measure of the value he attached to the marijuana smuggling, and not an important one at that. John received greater pleasure and reward from operating outside the law and from serving as a secret soldier in the IRA.

He originally offered to donate most of his share to

Secret Soldier

Ireland, but Murray ordered him to keep it. He then offered it to Robbi, the other object of his love, with whom he was still maintaining an off-again, on-again relationship. She eagerly accepted the mink coat John bought for her, but her greedy determination to live as well as the drug money would allow put John off. He refused her entreaties to buy a house. He didn't want to call attention to his wealth. Despite the gifts, he and Robbi were not getting along.

John finally decided to keep most of the two hundred thousand dollars he earned from smuggling hidden in a toolbox in his apartment in North Quincy. He did allow himself one small luxury—a new 1983 Buick Regal. He walked into a car dealership, spotted the car, and asked the salesman the price. They haggled a bit, and John inquired if the dealer accepted cash; the salesman said he did. John produced a Stop N Shop bag full of cash, handed it to the astonished man, got in the car, and drove off.

The car soon began to experience carburetor problems. The dealer, giving John the runaround, refused to fix it. So one day, John and Chuck, both dressed in jeans and borrowed black leather jackets, drove into the dealership. John carried an old German paratrooper's knife; one end had a marline-spike, the other a stiletto.

He tried politely to enlist the help of the salesman who had originally sold him the car, but got nowhere. So he snapped the blade out, put it up to the startled salesman's ear, and threatened, "You take care of me or I'm going to flay your fucking ear right here on the floor. You understand me?"

The dealer screamed uncontrollably for some moments— but he got the message. He showed John into the supervisor's office and arranged for the car to be fixed. When they got outside, John and Chuck dissolved into laughter. The crazy bluff had worked.

*　　*　　*

John was doing what he wanted to do. Nevertheless, as the months wore on without any indication of an arms shipment, he became uneasy about his life as a drug smuggler. At times, John felt there was no way out, that he had become a criminal rather than a partner in Ireland's liberation from British rule.

"I see a lot of silver going into your pocket, but I don't see any lead going across the ocean," complained John to Murray.

Joe kept putting John off, telling him he needed more money from drug profits before he could arrange a big weapons shipment to Ireland. Most of the funds, he kept telling John, were going to Mr. Big in Saint Augustine.

Although John didn't know it, thanks to his improvements in the drug-running system, Murray had become the biggest drug smuggler in New England. If for no other reason, Joe wanted to keep John happy. Soon, he promised, they would make history for the IRA.

John saw Murray just as he saw himself: a man of action for the Provos. He trusted Murray's promise of an arms shipment in 1984. He also found comfort in what he saw as the parallel between his actions and those of his father a generation earlier. Like him, John had enlisted to fight a black enemy. And just as his father had learned at Pullach, John too was discovering the unsavory truth that in order to fight evil, he had unwittingly allied himself with the devil.

5

A VISIT TO
THE FRONT

John believed Murray when he insisted that his involvement in the drug trade was restricted to smuggling marijuana through Walton's. The Feds, however, knew better. The marijuana represented only the tip of Joe Murray's burgeoning empire.

Toward the end of 1982, the FBI recruited someone close to Murray's confederate Joe Bangs as a confidential informant. The informant recalled hearing Bangs brag that in a couple of hours he had sold thirty thousand pounds of marijuana from the phone in Rascal's Bar in Boston. The bar was owned by a good friend of Joe Murray. The next month, the source reported that Bangs' partner met him at the bar; they went down to the cellar, where he saw them unloading shopping bags full of cash.

Not until March 1983, however, did the FBI develop a source that connected Bangs directly to Joe Murray. Some of Bangs' partners were busted by special agents of the Drug Enforcement Agency, which shared the drug beat in uneasy partnership with the FBI and U. S. Customs Service. Bangs, the Feds learned, was a big man in a heretofore unknown drug-smuggling organization run by Murray. They discovered that a shipment of marijuana was due to arrive in Boston within the next several weeks. DEA agents didn't know the location of the off-loading, but they learned that the consignment would be transferred to a warehouse in South Boston for distribution.

More often than not, the federal civil servants were more adept at prosecuting bureaucratic turf wars against their allies than at making a dent in the drug trade. Federal drug investigations in Massachusetts had degenerated into comic interservice rivalries. The FBI was contemptuous of the DEA, and both considered customs agents worse than inept. The Coast Guard complained that it lacked the funds to respond to every agency request for a ship to track down the smugglers who had invaded the New England shoreline. But the cry of poverty didn't impress veterans of similar budget battles at other agencies. Rival government agencies were not only prosecuting a war on drugs, but they were campaigning to upstage one another in the clamor for supremacy. Meanwhile, the real prey like Joe Bangs and his crowd were subject to only random surveillance by both the DEA and the FBI.

On April 6, 1983, the shreds of information collected by the FBI and DEA during the previous year unexpectedly came together. That day, Bangs was observed meeting Joe's brother, Michael Murray, and Joe Rooney at Santoro's sandwich shop on Northern Avenue.

Santoro's stands alone in a huge parking lot amid the sophisticated glitz of Boston's seaside renaissance, a tacky reminder of the seedy, often corrupt, workingman's haunts, which had once dominated the harbor front.

Where trading ships and seamen once ruled supreme, lawyers from the glass towers crowded onto State Street and secretaries from Government Center now enjoy lunch or a waterfront stroll. On this stretch of imported cobblestone and wood-planked boardwalks along Atlantic Avenue, polite cruises of Boston Harbor, a quick water taxi to Logan Airport

A Visit to the Front

across the way, and ferries to Nantasket Beach, Provincetown, and Gloucester cater to a world ignorant of the sea. The piers of Northern Avenue betray a different, more authentic kind of commerce, all that remains of Boston as seaport and shipyard. The Northern Avenue Bridge, an ancient collection of rusted steel girders, connects the revitalized stretch of wharfs along Atlantic Avenue with the working piers. There, tugs and trawlers compete for space along the docks. Even the Fan Pier, an empty expanse of landfill swinging into the harbor from the bridge, is being swallowed by real estate developers and seafood restaurants for the tourists.

Santoro's sits just up from the Fan Pier on Northern Avenue, where the cobblestones of another era have worn through the street pavement. It is a squat one-story concrete box, painted brown. A red hand-painted sign made from pieces of plywood has been strapped across the flat roof. The windows are barred, making the diners sitting on stools at the orange counter and looking out to the street appear more like convicts than patrons.

Bangs and Michael Murray left Santoro's for Murray's warehouse with the Feds trailing not far behind. The warehouse, a white cinder-block building with two large, garage-like black doors, was nearby in South Boston. About one-half hour after Bangs and Murray disappeared into it, one of the black doors opened and two vehicles—a green camper and a white truck—pulled out of the warehouse and drove back to Santoro's. Murray parked the truck on Northern Avenue and walked toward the diner. Joe Rooney walked from the diner toward Murray, and, as they passed, Murray slipped the truck's keys to him. Not a word was spoken between them nor a revealing gesture made. Rooney drove off to a garage in Dorchester, where agents arrested him and impounded his cargo of four thousand pounds of marijuana. With this evidence in hand, the Feds, working in concert for a change, easily convinced a judge to issue a search warrant for Mike Murray's warehouse, where they found several million dollars worth of Joe Murray's marijuana stacked in trailers.

The FBI and DEA agents congratulated one another on their great victory. Both the Murray brothers were under investigation for possession of saleable quantities of a controlled substance.

Michael Murray was no stranger to local law-enforcement agencies. The state police had wiretapped his liquor store in South Boston. The taps disclosed suspicious quantities and types of orders, more appropriate to cocaine distribution than liquor sales. Police recorded one customer complaining that two thousand dollars' worth of lobsters he had purchased had been dug up by his dog and eaten.

"You mean he ate two thousand dollars' worth of lobsters?" asked Murray's manager incredulously.

"Yeah," came the reply, "and he was staggering around shitting plastic bags all over the yard."

The Feds succeeded in shutting the doors to Murray's warehouse, but the source of the marijuana remained as elusive as ever. Had the drug hunters from the DEA and the FBI not been so greedy for a few kind words from the pundits, they could have bided their time and traced the operation from the warehouse in South Boston to its source at Walton's Pier. In the process, they would have developed an unchallengeable case against Joe Murray. As it was, the only evidence they had against Joe was his ownership of the warehouse and a single fingerprint on a ledger.

Gary Crossen had been prosecuting drug cases in the Boston office of the U. S. Attorney long enough to know this didn't amount to much of a case against Murray, but he was convinced that Joe was the key man in the operation. If he could get the case before a jury, Crossen was confident that Joe would be convicted.

John was at Robbi's apartment when he read about the bust in the next morning's paper. Joe, the paper reported, had been arrested and was free on bond. John was surprised to see that Joe's brother Mike was a partner in Joe's drug dealings— and shocked to discover how lucrative those dealings were.

John immediately went to Joe's house. After exchanging hurried pleasantries with Murray's wife, he and Joe closeted themselves in the kitchen.

John was furious about the bust. Murray had lied to him about his involvement in the distribution end. His greed had endangered the IRA's arms pipeline even before the first gun had been sent.

The top man in the Boston IRA, John said, was now a defendant in a drug case. If Joe's IRA connections became public, the drug bust would feed a media frenzy linking the IRA not only to terrorism but to drugs as well. Joe, John complained, completely disregarded his careful efforts to preserve security. John arranged the drug shipments so that they worked only one night each month, with a small crew to bring in the cargo. While the Coast Guard was chasing little boats up and down the coast, he succeeded month after month in safely transporting three hundred bales of grass at a time. It was now clear, however, that from the time the marijuana left Walton's, Murray had recklessly compromised the entire operation. Joe was dealing with the kind of mobsters and punks that John had all but purged from Walton's. Although the Feds had yet to catch on to the Chelsea end of the system, John argued, even they were bound to realize that the drugs found in the South Boston warehouse had to come from somewhere.

Joe, he said, had always insisted that he was nothing more than a middleman transporting drugs from one mob enterprise to another. Mr. Big in Florida, who organized importation and distribution, made the real money. This was the reason Joe lacked the funds to make John's sought-after arms shipment.

The warehouse bust exposed these excuses as a fraud.

The mysterious wholesaler siphoning the drug profits was none other than Joe Murray himself and his brother. According to the papers, Mike was making millions from marijuana distribution, but not one single bullet had been shipped to the Provos. Meanwhile, John was making the rounds of Southie's bars for Joe Murray on Saint Patrick's Day to collect nickels and dimes for the IRA, while the Murrays were collecting millions for themselves. John had been taken for a fool.

"I don't know who you work for, and I don't care," he said to his boss and IRA commander. "The drug smuggling stops now. I want to see some guns going to Ireland."

"Are you through?" Joe asked quietly. He understood why John was angry, he said, but there was no reason to place any blame on him.

Joe had an explanation for everything. He maintained that Crossen had nothing on him. His lawyers had already told him that he didn't have anything to worry about. True, he lied about the marijuana profits, but he had a good reason. His brother Mike was in trouble, and he wasn't the kind of guy to abandon family. Most importantly from John's point of view, Joe continued, there was no reason at all to worry about the safety of the marijuana pipeline John had worked so hard to establish and secure. It was impossible for the Feds to discover the drug-ferrying *D108*. Murray revealed that his source was a very senior official in the Coast Guard, a retired admiral with a soft spot for the IRA. The admiral and his network of IRA partisans on active duty kept an angel's eye on Murray's drug-importing operation. The admiral alerted Murray to the routes of Coast Guard drug patrols. Murray could easily plan his shipments for times and locations he could be certain would be safe. Sooner or later, every law-enforcement agency on the drug beat had to turn to the Coast Guard. And Murray had fixed it at the top. The *D108* operation was beyond the reach of the law.

John knew that Murray had a way of keeping the Walton's

A Visit to the Front

Pier operation out of harm's way, but he hadn't realized that Joe had penetrated the Coast Guard at such a senior level. He was impressed by Joe's connection, but these soothing words had no effect on John's insistent demands that Joe end the drug connection at Walton's and begin some concrete action on an arms transfer to Ireland. Joe was stung that John, formerly so trusting, was now determined to stand his ground.

Murray wasn't accustomed to taking orders from subordinates. He blustered a bit but knew John well enough to see that he had made up his mind. Joe took a deep .breath and agreed to an immediate end to the monthly drug runs. Walton's too, he promised, would be shut down before the Feds traced the marijuana trail.

Joe realized that he couldn't risk alienating John. He had, after all, been responsible for expanding Joe's marijuana operation over the previous fourteen months and the profits had helped Joe take financial control of even more lucrative drug operations. There was no reason that after a short hiatus they couldn't begin once again. And despite his greed, there was a part of Joe that was genuinely committed to sending the shipment of guns John now insisted upon.

John bought Walton a radio-controlled tugboat to pass the time in his new exile. He'd sit on the living-room sofa with a glass of brandy, puffing on a Pandora as he maneuvered the three-thousand-dollar toy around the indoor pool.

For $5 million Murray bought the pier, the *D108* barge, and the *Hudson* tugboat. He bridled at having to spend so much for what were, if only temporarily, useless assets. John arranged for the barge to be used for marine salvage, a legitimate but nonetheless profitable business. The tug was used for everyday marine towing.

Walton agreed to move his asbestos business to New Hampshire. Clayton Smith remained on the Chelsea payroll along with a few office clerks. Everything and everyone else would go—including Chris.

John had his brother fired. He told Chris not to bother about collecting unemployment benefits.

"Be a man about it," John instructed him. "Go and get another job, alright?" Chris trusted that John had a good reason for his advice. He had seen evidence himself that Walton's had become a dangerous place.

As John predicted, the Feds finally discovered Walton's Pier. In July 1983, he noticed a surveillance camera peering at the Chelsea Creek redoubt from a telephone pole on the other side of Marginal Street. For the Feds, however, the camera was too late. John had shut down the marijuana operation right after the April warehouse bust. Walton had long since moved away and the *Hudson* and *D108* were rolling listlessly at their moorings.

The U. S. Courthouse and Government Building is isolated by a ring of nondescript commercial buildings across the street from Boston's concrete and brick City Hall. The courthouse, a dour granite Federal structure with Doric columns and a tarnished copper roof, has been shoved by Boston's redevelopment into an anonymous canyon invisible from the street and inaccessible to all but the most adventurous. Once a centerpiece of Boston's public life, the courthouse today is overwhelmed by the glassy high-rise boxes where money and power rule.

The building houses the nerve center for the federal government's law-enforcement agencies in New England. Security is tight, with x-ray machines and armed U. S. Marshals guarding the elevator entrances to each of the federal courtrooms. The office of the U. S. Attorney has been secured by an additional barrier, a bulletproof partition through which all visitors are observed before they are permitted to enter the prosecutor's offices. Yet another security door, whose combi-

A Visit to the Front

nation is known only to the federal prosecutors and their staff, shields the Justice Department offices and files.

Gary Crossen, head of the Justice Department's regional criminal division, directed the investigation of Joe Murray from these offices. When the surveillance at Walton's turned up nothing, Crossen knew he would have to fight hard for a conviction. The only hard evidence he had connecting Joe Murray to his brother's warehouse was the single fingerprint found on a ledger.

It wasn't Crossen's fault that his case against Murray was so thin. He could only fire the ammunition that FBI and DEA agents gave him. Crossen was a good lawyer—honest, intelligent, and only too used to making the best of the limitations of a weak case. He managed to get a secret indictment, and on July 20, Murray was arrested by the FBI. The judge, however, preemptively dismissed the case against Joe on all counts, ending any prospect of the jury trial Crossen was counting upon. His brother Mike wasn't as lucky, but wound up with a relatively light three-year sentence.

Crossen was a professional, accustomed to taking his losses and moving on to the next case, but he and the investigators from the DEA and the FBI knew that Joe was a major player in New England's drug underworld. Informers said that Murray was now handling cocaine, hashish, counterfeit money, and worse. He had worked hard to build a case against Murray, and Crossen was angered by this setback. Jailing Joe Murray became a top priority.

The federal surveillance of Walton's vindicated not only John's demands made in the wake of the April bust, but also the campaign for greater security that he had waged for more than a year. Murray, who had only grudgingly listened to the pleadings of his protégé, was now forced to acknowledge the great debt he owed John for his caution and foresight. In the future, he would more readily accept John's advice.

When John spied the surveillance camera, he felt a certain ironic pride. It was too bad that Walton's had been located, he thought, but it could turn out to be the best thing that had happened to the Boston IRA in years. John was feeling increasingly powerful in his relationship with Murray. He no longer saw himself as a junior partner, constantly deferring on issues as important as the gun shipment to Ireland. Had John's warning not been heeded, Murray and the IRA's entire operation would have been fatally compromised. John now felt confident enough to conclude that Joe, if left to his own devices, was simply not capable of pulling off anything as sophisticated as gun smuggling.

John now understood how he had blinded himself to Murray's duplicity. He had been determined to prove that the nefarious world he had discovered at STRATCOM, and that his father and mother had discovered at Pullach, could be redeemed by Murray's campaign for Irish independence. At one time, Murray had been the personification of this noble struggle in John's world. But after the warehouse raid, John wondered how many other lies Murray had told him. Angered at Murray's double-dealing, John decided that it was now up to him to make the arms transfer happen.

During the summer and fall of 1983, John had a lot of time on his hands. Money was no problem; there was plenty left in his toolbox. He'd pass by Walton's, check on the salvage and pile-driving business he had established after Walton left, and shoot the breeze with Clayton. But he could usually be found with Murray, or hanging out at Heller's.

John had never given much thought to the economics of the smuggling trade. But when Joe easily came up with $5 million to retire Walton—money that he said came from the

106

A Visit to the Front

IRA arms war chest—a new and exciting horizon opened before him.

John had originally been won to drug smuggling by Murray's promise to send the proceeds to the IRA. Why not, thought John, make full use of Murray's Coast Guard connection to smuggle in vast quantities of marijuana—not merely enough to buy guns for an occasional shipment, but enough to finance a fully equipped Irish Republican Army that could take on the British army in a conventional war. The Coast Guard informant could be exploited so that they could safely import enough marijuana into the port of Boston to accomplish a first in the two-hundred-year struggle for Irish independence: the equipping of an Irish revolutionary army from abroad in complete secrecy.

John saw himself as the key to this historic undertaking. Just as Murray had eased Walton out, John would now use the connections that Murray had established to create, under John's direction, a secure marijuana-for-cash-for-arms pipeline to the IRA. Ireland would be redeemed, as would John's decision to fight for its freedom.

John outlined to Murray a plan far more brazen than the multimillion-dollar barge-tug operation. He proposed that the IRA buy a freighter, fill it with marijuana destined for the Mob, and hire a British crew to sail it right into Boston Harbor. There would be no transfer from the mother ship, no off-load at sea, no lumpers, ropers, or pilots with dubious loyalties. The mother ship itself would enter the harbor and dock at a secure yard, ostensibly for repairs or salvage. There it would remain as a floating warehouse. Trusted IRA soldiers would dump the marijuana into cargo containers dropped out of sight into the hold. The filled containers would then be lifted by crane onto waiting tractor-trailer trucks for distribution by the Mob.

John had two questions for Murray. Could the IRA buy a

freighter? And could Murray locate a secure shipyard on the Boston waterfront?

Murray was impressed by the audacity of John's idea, and he chuckled at the irony of British sailors ferrying a cargo destined to pay for IRA guns. Ever since Walton's shut down, the Mafia had suffered one failure after another in its efforts to find an alternate route into Boston Harbor. John's plan would open a secure pipeline for the Mob and generate enough money to satisfy both Joe's greed and the most outrageous demands of the IRA. John dangled the promise of huge drug profits before Murray; Murray opened his mouth wide and swallowed it whole.

Joe suggested that John speak with a local mobster and business associate, about finding a suitable shipyard in East Boston. Before year's end, he promised there would be a freighter waiting for John's command.

John needed Murray to make this operation work, but he would no longer be content with mere promises of future action. The new scheme, he told Joe, would begin only after they had delivered Murray's long-promised shipment of arms to Ireland.

Murray readily agreed. He had already decided to make a delivery in 1984, so he had no problem with John's itinerary. But Murray was smart enough to understand that John needed a bit of pampering after the warehouse bust and the discovery of Walton's.

Joe offered John the sweetest deal he could think of. If John would agree to supervise the smuggling operation he had outlined, Murray would arrange for John to travel underground with him to Ireland to coordinate the shipment for the Provos. There, John would take personal responsibility for the transport's security.

Murray rightly knew that John would jump at the chance to play the undercover game. John harbored doubts about Murray and was easily convinced that he should be the Provos'

A Visit to the Front

operational contact with the Boston IRA. This rational consideration, however, paled against the excitement John felt when Murray offered him the chance to be smuggled into Belfast to see firsthand the fight for a free Ireland. It was one thing to read about Ireland and to croon tributes to the Irish in Boston bars. It was another thing entirely to join in the fray. At last, John would get the chance to do for Ireland what his father had done for the free world—and what John had tried to do for his own country. Like his grandfather, he would stand up to tyranny. At last, John would take his romanticized journey into the underworld of spies and false passports, where daring and courage were measured in life and death. He couldn't wait to get started.

John and Joe flew to Amsterdam in January 1984. Customs agents in Boston noted their departure but lacked both the resources and inclination to take further action. John and Joe were joined on the plane by Pat Nee, Murray's IRA confederate from South Boston. Nee had seen combat in Vietnam and knew firsthand the range of supplies and hardware required to equip a crack military outfit. The weapons delivery was to be the first joint Southie-Charlestown IRA operation.

John arrived in Amsterdam on the morning of January 11 and headed directly for the waterfront to meet the contacts Murray had set up. He was taken to a shipyard where a rusty freighter, the *Ramsland*, was moored. Docked next to it was the *Marita Ann*, the trawler that would ferry John's arms shipment from the Boston ship to Ireland.

The *Ramsland* was a nondescript freighter, over two hundred feet long, black above the waterline with a white two-story pilot house at her stern. John climbed aboard and surveyed the vessel. Below deck, he measured the compartments along her keel ordinarily used for oil and ballast.

John explained to the workmen how to construct a duplicate fuel tank and weld it parallel to the keel. This new container would be more than adequate for the forty tons of marijuana the *Ramsland* would carry on its test run into Boston. After installing the tank, the workmen were to lay a thin layer of sand and gravel over the *Ramsland*'s entire interior hold, covering the expanded keel with its new secret compartment. To any official who boarded her, she would appear to be an empty freighter in need of a cleaning. Even if the gravel was removed and the keel's storage units examined, no one would think to look for a second unit welded alongside.

John then turned his attention to the *Marita Ann.*

"It's a pleasure," exclaimed her captain Michael Browne, as John stepped aboard. "From what we've heard about you, you're the American admiral of the IRA."

John thanked him for the compliment. He examined the rigging quickly but with care, climbed up on her booms, and checked the strength of the block and tackle. He issued some instructions to Browne and was on his way. Barely a few hours after his arrival in Amsterdam, John was off once again. His destination: Ireland.

The IRA spirited John, Murray, and Nee in a small twin-engine airplane from Amsterdam to the seaside village of Fenit on Ireland's western coast. John's adrenaline was pumping when he arrived. This was the life he was made for. At long last, he had joined the ranks of unsung undercover patriots.

At Fenit, John met their Provo contact, Sean Crawley, a former Navy SEAL now enlisted in the IRA. Sean, twenty-seven, was born in the United States but immigrated to Ireland as a child. He later returned to Chicago, where he completed high school, and then joined the Navy SEALS, an elite commando force. After concluding his military service in the late seventies, Sean returned to Ireland and the IRA.

John, although merely Joe's lieutenant, clearly had the firmest grasp of the details of the operation. He had instructed

A Visit to the Front

Murray to establish only a single IRA contact, who in turn reported directly to the ruling IRA Army Council. That day, the five men reviewed the logistics of off-loading the arms at Fenit and transferring them to the IRA training compound near the Northern Ireland border. Nee and Crawley were to run this camp where skilled military attacks on British outposts were to be prepared.

At their meeting, the Army Council representative passed along the IRA'S wish list of military supplies to Murray for safekeeping and to the military professionals Nee and Crawley for review and comment. Previous attempts had been made to smuggle huge arsenals; this time, the shipment would be small enough to fit on a single small trawler.

The transfer, continued the IRA contact, was a matter of some urgency. The organization hadn't received a shipment of comparable size in more than a decade. Matériel was in such short supply that bomb detonators were being made from condoms.

No specific date for the transfer was agreed upon beyond Murray's commitment to make a shipment before year's end. To John, this meant that the guns would have to depart Boston by the end of September at the latest, before the hurricane season made the North Atlantic passage too treacherous.

After their business was done, the IRA operative led the Americans on a hike into the Irish countryside. John wasn't prepared for the land's misty beauty. Even in the dead of winter, it had a haunting character. Like a lace veil, the perennial fog hid its blemishes, leaving only an elegant profile.

Murray asked John to take a picture of him and the three others when they reached the top of a hill. From where he stood, John looked north into the northern four counties, the next stop on his whirlwind journey.

John was smuggled across the border and into Northern Ireland for a firsthand look at the people and the land he was fighting for. The stealth amused him; the sense of danger thrilled him. He felt the ghosts of laughing Irish rebels, and perhaps the encouraging smile of his father as well, as he walked past a pair of British sentries patrolling the streets.

Guides took him to Belfast's Lower Falls Road, the heart of the Catholic ghetto. The poverty and brutal evidence of British oppression stunned him. British Saracens, armored personnel carriers, roamed the burnt-out streets, leaving no doubt in John's mind that he had entered a war zone.

The Belfast Provo command knew that John was an American VIP, and they wanted to show him what American money was paying for. They told him of a daylight ambush they had planned and invited him along. But after several hours' wait, the leader called off the operation and led his men to the nearest pub. John laughed to himself that this was a hell of a way to fight a war: everyone quits shooting at five o'clock to have a pint.

The pathetic state of the Provo arsenal was partly to blame. The British had been very effective at shutting off new arms infusions to the rebels. The money collected in the States was earmarked by NORAID, the Northern Ireland Aid Committee, for civilian relief. The tens of millions of Irish descendants in the United States donated less than half a million dollars to the IRA's military stockpile. John saw the results of this neglect—an arsenal empty except for a handful of automatic rifles, a few pistols, and one machine gun in desperate need of repair. The kids in the streets who threw stones and Molotov cocktails at the Saracens, he mused, stood a better chance of surviving combat than did the ill-equipped soldiers of the IRA.

At the pub, John listened sympathetically to laments about the daily life of the Catholics in Northern Ireland. Between beers, the locals explained that they were an oppressed minority in their own country. Civil rights were nonexistent, and the courts were stacked against them. Sus-

A Visit to the Front

pected IRA members were denied jury trials and the right to confront their accusers. The word of a supergrass—as the British called an informer—was enough for a conviction by a British judge. A honest word offered by a Catholic, on the other hand, was never good enough, they complained. Catholics were the niggers of Belfast, John was told. They had no say, no vote, no jobs, and no justice in the land of their birth.

John bristled at this analogy. Bigotry was a fact of life down at Walton's. Racial epithets unfashionable in the suburbs were common currency in Chelsea and Charlestown.

John had always been blind to such distinctions. One evening two black men made the mistake of walking into the Port o'Call, a bar crowded with young people from Quincy. Both were marine sergeants, but they were unable to fight off the pack of drunken toughs that held them up and ripped off their medals. John noticed that both marines wore the insignia of Vietnam veterans, and he jumped to their defense. When John fought, he knew no limitations. He scattered the bullies, enabling the marines to make their getaway. John had no use for bigots.

And what of Ireland's children? They looked at the lives of their unemployed parents and broken grandparents and knew in their hearts that their turn would never come. They had no hope, no faith in a better future.

It was these soulful kids who shocked John the most. They were angry, dirty, uneducated, ill fed and frightened about facing the world day after day—and not without reason. The contrast with his own youth was painfully obvious. He had enjoyed such a wonderful childhood, filled with family trips, dances, and parties, where the only limitations to enjoyment were those he imposed upon himself. These kids would never know such pleasures or such freedom, he told himself, unless someone forced a change.

The indifferent faces of these children brought back memories of the death of his childhood friend. A visit to a Catholic orphanage, with its pathetic playroom and cracked windows, overwhelmed him. There he found children whose parents had been lost to the war, kids whose families were denied to them forever. The authorities had little sympathy for the children of IRA rebels. Theirs was the sin of birth, and the punishment exacted was the loss of their youth and their future.

In this great and civilized British Commonwealth festered a scandal out of Dickens, thought John. Injustice had run amok, and innocent children had been made prisoners in their own country.

The toddlers climbed onto his lap. John had a way with children, open and unaffected. He made them laugh, but their big, sad eyes broke his heart.

These innocents, John decided, were the cause that fate called upon him to embrace. Their suffering justified the battle he waged. All doubt about Murray and misgivings about the drug smuggling vanished before John's witness to the misery of these kids. Their pain was his pain.

John emptied his money belt of thousands in cash and donated it to the orphanage on the spot. He gave his money like he offered his loyalty: willingly, impetuously, and full of hope that it would bring immediate good. He left the orphanage feeling more secure than ever that he was a warrior in an honorable crusade.

On January 15, John was smuggled out of Ireland and back to Amsterdam, where he caught a flight that same day to JFK. As he made his way over the wintry Atlantic, all his thoughts were of Ireland's children and his hope for their liberty. But before Ireland could be free, John and the Boston IRA needed to supply its soldiers with guns.

6

~~~~~~

MAKING READY

Assembling the arsenal on the IRA wish list was Murray's responsibility. Joe, like John, was no stranger to firearms. He'd been licensed in Massachusetts to carry a concealed handgun in 1970; over the years, he had amassed a personal collection of rifles, shotguns, and pistols purchased from local outlets. During the off-loads at Walton's, he could often be seen carrying a silencer-equipped 9mm gun.

Pat Nee, head of the Provos' South Boston section, worked with Joe to put the shipment together. For Nee, as for Murray, the IRA was only a sideline. He boasted a criminal record stretching back almost twenty years, including allegations running from assault with intent to murder to breaking and entering and possession of a firearm.

Sean Crawley was seconded by the Provos to be Murray's munitions expert. Crawley was the ultimate IRA operative, quiet and unassuming. He looked more a student, with his gold-rimmed glasses and curly brown hair, than a dedicated commando, schooled in the art of sabotage and assassination. According to Joe, no one was more willing than Sean to risk his life for the cause.

Murray had a supply of automatic rifles—still in their cases—that had been stolen by the Mob from an Ohio National Guard armory. But he needed more guns, as well as ammunition and other military and surveillance equipment, to fulfill the requirements on the IRA wish list. The Provos could make Joe's life very uncomfortable indeed if he didn't deliver on their request.

Murray wasn't a professional gun smuggler. What guns he and his confederates couldn't steal, Joe decided to buy on the open market, from established, legitimate companies. Military suppliers across the country willingly sold him missile warheads, machine-gun manuals, rockets, and enough ammunition to start a small war. Accompanying each sale, however, was a small mountain of paperwork. In the months after their return from Ireland, Murray and Nee left a trail of purchases so clumsy that even Inspector Clousseau could have tripped across it.

On April 3, Nee mailed an order for three missile warheads to the Barnacle Wharf Trading Company in Newark, Ohio. When ordering, Nee used the alias Patrick Mullen, as he did for all subsequent purchases for the shipment. He asked that the items be sent via UPS to Mullen at the Columbia Yacht Club in South Boston, where Nee was a member.

Nee paid for the warheads with a bank money order. In every instance where Nee bought supplies with bank checks, he purchased those checks with cash from banks that had no camera surveillance and at which he had no account. Nevertheless, bank requirements also established a paper trail that investigators would eventually be able to mine for information about the smuggling scheme.

On April 9, Sierra Supply in Durango, Colorado, received a mail order for miscellaneous weapons manuals. Delivery instructions were the same—UPS to Patrick Mullen at the Columbia Yacht Club. The manuals arrived at the CYC on April 20.

On April 10, the Jolly Roger Surplus Company in Pennsylvania received a mail order for five cases of .50-caliber ammunition cans. The shipment was delivered to the South Boston address on April 12.

On April 11, Murray and Nee drove Murray's Blazer to the Numrich Arms Company in West Hurley, New York, a small town in the Catskills. Nee, using the Mullen alias, said he wanted to make some purchases for the boys at the gun club—Vietnam veterans who had pooled their money and given him a shopping list of gun supplies. Nee bought one thousand ammo clips for M-16 automatic rifles, one hundred rifle covers, and fifty side-mount ammunition cans. He ordered the equipment sent to the Columbia Gun and Yacht Club—an interesting combination, which, however, raised no suspicions at Numrich, or anywhere else for that matter. Murray was paying cash, and Numrich and the others were in business to sell. Nee left identifiable fingerprints all over the order form.

On April 17, Nee mailed a $2,112 money order to a California arms dealer for two hundred Rhodesian pouches. These are worn like a vest and are made to be concealed under a jacket. Each pouch contains pockets capable of holding 150 rounds of ammunition, more than enough firepower for the IRA soldiers Nee would soon be training at the secret base in Ireland. Enclosed with the payment was a note requesting that the order be air shipped to the CYC.

Dennis Ronan, the CYC steward, used a number of unimaginative aliases when signing for the packages addressed to the equally fictitious Pat Mullen. The boxes delivered by UPS sat untended in the hallway, piled next to the cigarette machine, until Pat Nee picked them up.

On one occasion, UPS delivered a package addressed to Patrick Mullen, Commodore of the CYC. Returning to the club on a subsequent delivery, the UPS carrier was asked to route the envelope to Nee's home address in South Boston. To someone at the CYC, it was no secret that Pat Mullen was really Pat Nee.

Only once during their cross-country sweep were Murray and Nee turned away by a gun shop. On June 1, Sarco, Inc., in Newark, New Jersey, received a $2,000 down payment from Nee, followed a week later by an additional $3,000 deposit on a long list of military items valued at $22,716. On June 29, Nee, Murray, and two grunts showed up at Sarco's in two vehicles. At one point, Nee considered purchasing ten cases of 9mm ammunition but balked when asked to produce some positive identification as required by law. Nee told one of the two men loading the equipment to produce a driver's license instead. The clerk, however, refused to accept the proffered Arizona license, which he suspected was counterfeit. Nee decided to pass on the ammunition. He paid the balance, approximately $18,000, in cash, loaded the supplies into the two vehicles, and drove off.

In addition to the matériel Nee ordered, Murray assembled almost one hundred weapons from the Ohio National Guard armory, a large number of military-surplus firearms, and a kilo of the construction explosive cordite procured by Sean through his contacts across the country.

Joe also did some of his own freelancing to fill out the arsenal. On at least six occasions between May 2 and August 24, Joe himself made the rounds of Boston-area gun shops, spending seven thousand dollars in cash for the purchase of one dozen military assault rifles destined for the IRA. Incredibly, he registered these guns in his own name.

On May 2, he bought a Heckler and Koch .308-caliber assault rifle and a Colt AR-15 rifle from Ivanhoe's in Watertown. A month later, he purchased two more Heckler and Koch rifles from the same outfit. On June 15, he bought two additional Colt rifles, this time from Roache's in Cambridge. Four days later, he acquired another Colt and a Heckler and Koch, along with large quantities of ammunition and electronic gun sights, from the Collector's Coin Gallery in Stoneham.

Every one of these purchases was registered with the Firearms Division of the Massachusetts Department of Public Safety. On the official order forms, Joe listed the *Boston Globe* as his employer, where he claimed to work as a printer. Joe's only nod to security was to use three different addresses, two in Charlestown and one in Boston. For one sale, Joe began to write a Charlestown address but crossed it out in favor of the Boston location. It wasn't every day that Joe forgot where he lived. He was just trying to beat the bureaucrats at their own game.

On June 27, Murray purchased a Steyr .308 semiautomatic rifle from Roache's. This weapon, a favorite of snipers, would be the first gun found aboard the *Marita Ann* that the Bureau of Alcohol, Tobacco and Firearms would be able to positively trace to Joe Murray.

As late as August 24, less than three weeks before the *Valhalla* sailed, Murray was still adding to his collection with the purchase of yet another Heckler and Koch from Ivanhoe's. Among the rifles seized aboard the *Marita Ann* were twenty-three Colt AR-15s and thirteen Heckler and Koch rifles. All of the serial numbers had been filed off, but the guns were consistent with the make, model, and caliber of weapons personally purchased by Murray and traced by the Bureau of Alcohol, Tobacco and Firearms.

Murray even enlisted some of Boston's finest in his arms spending spree that summer. MDC Patrolman Michael Hanley and his partner Charles Tourkantonis often stopped by Murray's garage on Warren Street in Charlestown for a cup of coffee. While having coffee one day in late May, Murray introduced Sean to the two officers. Sean said he was a marine veteran, and Hanley, like most old soldiers, was happy to swap stories with another marine. Sean explained that he and some friends were planning to make a pleasure trip to Ireland, but they were concerned for their safety. How, he asked casually, could he buy some bulletproof vests? Sean's new friend Hanley promised to see how such a purchase could be made.

The next time they met over coffee, Hanley offered to make the buy himself. The cops later insisted that they didn't suspect anything illegal about the request for bulletproof vests from Joe Murray's young Irish friend on his way to the mother country.

On June 14, Murray, Sean, and Pat Nee accompanied the cops to the Professional Image Uniform Company in Woburn. Hanley ordered ten vests and paid the $3,550 bill with cash provided by Sean. Once again, Nee left his prints on the order form. On July 5, the cops picked up the order and dutifully delivered it to Murray's Towing Company in Charlestown. The vests, their serial numbers still intact, were found aboard the *Marita Ann* by the Irish police.

In addition to the cache of weapons stolen from the Ohio armory and those acquired by Murray and Sean, twenty-five guns stolen from as far away as Chicago over a twenty-five year period were ferried to Murray's Maine vacation house in Belgrade Lakes, midway between Augusta and Skowhegan, where the military stockpile was being assembled. A Remington semiautomatic 12-gauge shotgun stolen from Medford and a Smith and Wesson .45-caliber revolver traced to a 1959 theft in Brookline were included in this category.

In addition, two of the six Ruger Mini-14 rifles confiscated aboard the *Marita Ann* were traced to two men in Detroit. Both had been investigated in 1973 and again in 1976 for arms trafficking to Ireland.

By Labor Day, Murray had assembled a motley but lethal arsenal: 34 revolvers, 87 semiautomatic rifles, 17 semiautomatic pistols, 6 bolt-action rifles, 5 pump-action shotguns, 8 submachine guns, 3 lever-action rifles, 1 derringer, and one double-barreled shotgun. The serial numbers of eighty-six of the firearms were still intact. Murray, at John's direction, had also acquired debugging equipment and voice-distorting devices aimed at increasing the protection afforded to the IRA's notoriously insecure communications. All they lacked was a boat.

When John returned from Amsterdam in January, he had two ships—the *Ramsland* and the *Marita Ann*. He needed a third to transport the arms shipment Murray was assembling from the United States to the rendezvous off the coast of Ireland.

"Here's how it can work. All we need is a boat with these dimensions, rigged for side dragging," explained John to Brendan Kelly. Kelly was a good friend of John's. They had met at the waterfront, where Kelly did some part-time work for Murray. Kelly was about John's age and a good seaman. He stayed away from drug smuggling, however, because his brother drowned on one of LePere's unseaworthy trawlers.

John wanted a boat that was truly outfitted for fishing, one that would dispel any suspicion that she was engaged in anything but dragging for a catch.

"Do you think that you can find one?" he asked Kelly.

Kelly went to Clayton Smith, John's old friend from Walton's Pier. Clayton knew of a big side-dragging trawler, the *Surge*, that had been for sale for several years. At 150 feet long, she could make an Atlantic crossing in any weather, and she carried enough diesel to make the round-trip passage without refueling. But she had been laying unheated in Portland, Maine, and the bitter winter weather had frozen much of her machinery. John asked Clayton to stop by the *Surge* on his way from Boston to his home in northern Maine to see if he could get her engine started. After much effort, Clayton coaxed the motor to life.

On March 14, John laundered the money needed to buy the old trawler. He sent a courier on a tour of the Bank of New England's Boston offices, making three cash deposits of $9,000 and one of $8,000, each at a different branch. John wanted to skirt the requirement that banks report every cash transaction of $10,000 or more. The total sum of $35,000 was deposited in the account of Black Creek Marine Towing and Construction, a front company owned by John. John had earlier used Black Creek to purchase the old tug *Hudson* from Walton.

One day later, John arranged for the *Surge* to be purchased by Black Creek with a certified check for $35,000 made out to the *Surge*'s owners, B and B Trawlers. On paper, at least, it seemed an innocuous, legal deal.

John and Brendan piloted the *Surge* from Portland to the nearby National Sea Products shipyard in Rockland, where the boat was hauled out of the water and its bottom was scraped and repainted.

When these repairs were completed, John, Clayton, and Brendan made the overnight trip down the coast to Boston Harbor. Because of the surveillance still in force at Walton's, the *Surge* was moored at the Fish Pier off Northern Avenue, where repairs to the boat would not attract any attention. Clayton moved his tools over from Walton's and set to the restoration. He was the only real fisherman among them who knew how to outfit the *Surge* for offshore dragging.

John would have preferred to have invested more than $35,000 for a ship with such an important mission, but Murray refused to spend money on an asset that wouldn't make him a buck.

Murray got just what he had paid for. The *Surge* was a mess.

"Almost everything you laid your hands on," recalled Clayton, "had to be replaced or worked on, one or the other."

Clayton repaired the large winch at the trawler's stern and all of the blocks. He spliced all the towing wires and set up a single dragger for fishing. Clayton knew, though, that the rigging he was repairing was just a sideshow. He had no doubt that the *Surge* was going to be pressed into the drug-smuggling business.

Sean Crawley, the coordinator of the IRA armaments shopping list, doubled as a painter. Clayton found him to be smarter and more diligent than the customary waterfront lowlifes. This soft-spoken kid with an Irish brogue seemed unusual to Clayton, and he tried without success to draw Sean into conversation.

During the entire time Clayton worked on the *Surge*, he never strayed into the fish hole, which was often filled with the din of heavy construction. John wasn't preparing the hold for fish but for the weapons that would be secreted in a newly constructed false compartment.

Joe Murray visited the *Surge* almost daily. He'd argue with Clayton about his slow progress and complain to John about the steadily escalating bills. Repairs were costing a small fortune, a good part of which Joe suspected went to pay Kelly's gambling losses, not repair work. Murray also suspected that Clayton's slow pace was a deliberate attempt to squeeze him for as much money as possible. The marijuana operation had been shut down for a year, and the drug profits wouldn't begin to flow again until the arms transfer came off and the *Ramsland* was brought in to Boston.

John attempted to mollify Joe. He explained that the *Surge* hadn't been moved in three years. Everything on board was rusted. The entire deck needed replacing and the engine required extensive and unanticipated repairs, all of which were adding up to much more than the $35,000 Murray had already invested.

John didn't want to tell Joe that he too was frustrated at the slow pace of the *Surge*'s rehabilitation. It was almost July, they'd been working on the vessel since April, and there was no end in sight. John too had had a number of disagreements with Clayton. Even in the best of times, Clayton never liked to work fast. Now he constantly argued with John about his timetable, wondering why Sean, for example, was painting the aft cabins before they had solved the engine's major problems.

Clayton sustained a leg injury one day in late June, slowing his pace even further. The sore ulcerated, and Clayton could hardly walk for the pain, let alone continue his repair of the *Surge*'s antiquated engine. He told John he was taking a couple of weeks off to let the wound heal.

John was working against an IRA deadline and could not tolerate any further delay in making the ship ready. Without Clayton's help, there was no chance that the *Surge* could be made seaworthy in time.

John protested that Clayton couldn't just walk off the job. Clayton, his frustration building after weeks of bullying, had reached his limit. He announced that he was leaving immediately to have his injury examined and he would return when he was ready.

Clayton stomped off the dock, too angry to remember that he was leaving his expensive welding and rigging tools behind.

Perhaps Clayton's abrupt departure was a blessing. There was just too much wrong with the *Surge*, John decided. Another boat would have to be found and fast if there was to be any likelihood of a shipment before year's end.

John told Murray of Clayton's hasty exit. The *Surge*'s engine, even when fixed, might still not be able to make the trip to the Irish coast. Joe, he warned, would have a lot to account for if that happened. A more reliable and expensive replacement would have to be found quickly if they hoped to meet the September deadline.

Murray didn't need John to tell him that the *Surge* was a money-sucking black hole. He bridled at the thought of yet another investment, but he realized that it would be best to cut his losses. Another boat would have to be found, but this time, one of his friends would select it.

Making Ready

Murray ordered John to sell the *Surge* immediately. There was no reason, he thought, to have two boats when one would do.

John disagreed. He explained that the *Surge* offered good cover for their operation should snoopy Feds or British-intelligence agents have them under surveillance. All they would see would be a half-completed ship in full view at the Fish Pier. John argued that it also made sense to keep a small crew puttering around the *Surge* at its Boston mooring while the yet-to-be-purchased new boat was secretly outfitted elsewhere.

Murray agreed that John could hold on to the *Surge* at the Fish Pier and even keep on a couple of workmen for appearance's sake. But for his next purchase, Murray wanted to get as far away from Boston as he could. He called Bob Anderson, an old friend who had worked as a captain for Frankie LePere, and a meeting was arranged at Murray's home.

For more than a year, Murray's Charlestown address had been under casual surveillance by the joint FBI, DEA, and customs Federal Drug Task Force, the same group that had handled the warehouse bust. Although Murray had been acquitted, the Feds had no doubt that he was a key drug importer. They suspected that this get-together between Anderson and Murray, like the previous ones they had recorded between Murray and various felons throughout the year, was far from innocent. Anderson too was suspect. His boat the *Kristen Lee* had been confiscated in 1981 when Anderson was convicted for catching swordfish illegally. There was also evidence, gleaned from an informant, that the captain was deeply involved in narcotics trafficking.

The July meeting convinced the Feds that Murray was getting careless and was planning yet another pot-smuggling operation with Anderson. They had no idea that the subject of his July meeting with Anderson was guns, not drugs. This time, unlike the warehouse bust, the Feds were determined not to act too hastily. They left Anderson and Murray alone, devoting scarce resources to peripheral figures in Joe's organization instead. One person, for example, was indicted in September on a four-year-old smuggling charge connected with the Feds' clean-up of the long-defunct LePere organization. But the agents' casual surveillance missed Murray's harried summer rounds of area gun shops and his interstate trips with Nee and Crawley. Once again, the Feds had missed the motherlode and were mining a little vein. That summer, Murray offered federal investigators an open invitation to arrest; the Feds proved more inept than he.

"Do you think that it's big enough?" John asked Anderson. The vessel put up for auction by the U. S. Marshals was a trawler like the *Surge*, but barely half its size.

"It will get you there and back," promised Anderson.

"Then let's bid on it," said John, hopeful that the captain's claims about the boat's reliability were accurate.

On that steamy July day, the government of the United States sold Bob Anderson the old *Kristen Lee*—the very boat it had confiscated from him some years earlier. Leeward, a new company fronting for Joe Murray, paid close to a quarter of a million dollars for her. Joe Murray could not object since John and his friends paid for it out of their own pockets.

The U. S. Marshals Service had no idea of the connection established between Murray and Anderson only days earlier. No one from the Federal Drug Task Force had informed them. In any case, tracking down drug deals before they happened wasn't their mandate. The U. S. Marshals office was paid to sell confiscated drug boats—they didn't care much to whom.

Anderson thanked the auctioneer. Then, turning to John, he said, "It's your boat now. Gotta name for 'er?"

John smiled. There was only one name appropriate for this ship.

"*Valhalla,*" he announced without hesitation, remembering the boat of his youth.

The *Surge* had cost John valuable time. Now he had one year of repairs on the *Valhalla* to make in less than forty-five days.

During the last week of July, Anderson made arrangements with Gloucester Marine Railways to receive the *Valhalla* for extensive repairs. Anderson was a regular customer at GMR; the workmen were familiar with the vessel, which had been in for refitting when it was the *Kristen Lee*.

On August 1, the ship was towed from its berth in East Boston to the GMR dry dock on the harbor side of the single pier. GMR was a small enterprise operating out of a single-story white cinder-block building right next to the U. S. Coast Guard station, a squat red-brick building sitting on a bluff dominating the southern shore of Gloucester Harbor.

Over the next month, John supervised over thirty thousand dollars' worth of repairs on the *Valhalla*. Because the ship had been laid up since it had been seized from Anderson, there was much to restore. Water had to be pumped out of the fuel tanks. Expensive ultrasound tests had to be made to determine whether any structural damage had occurred while it was in the U. S. Marshals' custody. On August 15, after sandblasting and painting the hull, supplying new bearings for the engine shaft, and repairing the transducer, GMR launched the boat, now formally renamed the *Valhalla*.

As she sat in the water, the *Valhalla*'s fish pens and coolers were sandblasted and mended. John didn't have time to build secret compartments like those he had installed on the *Surge*. The weapons would simply have to be stored in the fish pens.

John spent workdays and weekends making needed improvements on the boat. Everything, it seemed, had to be made right. He hired one crew to tear out all of the old electronic equipment on board and had another repair the water pumps. John kept a meticulous ledger of daily expenses and parts replaced, often noting that he paid a premium for fast service.

By the end of August, John was sending Kelly to buy food for the long voyage. He had drawn up the menu himself. It was typical fisherman's fare—simple food heavy on starches and protein—ham and eggs for breakfast, baloney and cheese sandwiches for lunch, spaghetti or meat loaf for dinner, and plenty of canned vegetables and fruits. Alcoholic beverages were conspicuously absent.

If the fare was Spartan, the safety measures were deluxe. John had once been hit by a towering rogue wave during a nor'easter off the coast of Maine. The storm sunk his boat, and were it not for the survival suits he had on board, John and the two other crewmen would have drowned.

John purchased the best survival rafts and suits and the latest in marine communications and navigational electronics, includng two Lorans. This equipment would enable Anderson to rendezvous with the *Marita Ann* in any kind of weather.

GMR fitted the *Valhalla* with stabilizing outriggers on both port and starboard sides. They would help provide stability for navigating in high seas.

John replaced the ship's cracked wheelhouse windows with special glass shields. These circular panels were several inches thick and cost many thousands of dollars, but they would protect the bridge and its bank of sensitive electronics from everything but the meanest rogue wave.

By the first week in September, the *Valhalla* was ready. John had thrown heart and soul into meeting the deadline set in Ireland eight months earlier. As the date for the *Valhalla*'s journey approached, John excitedly told Chris about his imminent departure. Chris suspected right away that John was up to more than just fishing.

Making Ready

Chris had returned to school the fall after he had left Walton's. His life was now far removed from the rhythm of the waterfront. His world revolved around books and exams; John's life of covert intrigue no longer held any attraction. Chris didn't try to ask John what the enterprise was really about. He knew his brother too well for that.

"Good luck," was all that Chris said. "You're going to need it."

When the time came to transport the guns to Gloucester, Murray organized a small convoy of vehicles to make the run from his Maine summer house where the arsenal was stored. It took two trips of the fleet—Joe's Chevy Blazer, a black Chevy pickup, and a Dodge van owned by Nee—to ferry to Gloucester the seven tons of weapons and supplies acquired since April.

The repair work to the *Valhalla* was consistent with Anderson's cover story to GMR that she was being outfitted for swordfishing, which often required boats to be offshore for up to five weeks at a time. From the fifty-seven tons of ice in the fish hold to the reconstructed power winch off the transom, John had gone to great expense to lend credibility to the subterfuge of an extended offshore fishing expedition. Except for the load of guns on board, the *Valhalla* could just as easily hunt for swordfish off Newfoundland as for the *Marita Ann* off Porcupine Bank.

After their arguments about the *Surge*, Murray ordered John to keep Clayton off the *Valhalla*'s repair crew. He was suspicious of the old man's nitpicking repairs and didn't want him near the boat. Murray believed that Clayton would bill him for a total overhaul, if given half a chance.

Clayton realized that he had been kept in the dark about the *Surge* and made a point of trying to find out about the *Valhalla*'s progress. He knew from bits of information gleaned from John and others that the *Valhalla* was being readied for an IRA mission; beyond that he knew no details of the transfer. His feelings were hurt at being shut out. Clayton told John that he wanted to make the trip, but Murray refused to consider it. Clayton, he insisted to John, was too old for such a demanding voyage.

John was well aware of Joe's unspoken concerns. To Joe, Clayton's history of repair delays seemed almost like sabotage. But John trusted Clayton, perhaps more than he trusted anyone on the waterfront. However, he didn't quarrel with Joe's decision. Joe still called the shots.

On the morning of September 13, John told his parents he was going on an extended fishing trip. But if anyone asked, particularly Clayton, John told them to say only that he was off drinking with some buddies and he would be back in a day or two. He had conveyed the same request to Robbi. John liked Clayton, but what if Murray was right?

John's father believed that he had a special intuition about John, particularly when it involved his mischievous escapades. On more than one occasion, he'd driven to Chelsea Creek to search for him. He'd pull out his binoculars and scan the piers for some sign of his son. More often than not, he'd find him. A heart condition was making these surreptitious forays more difficult, but he still prided himself on the sixth sense that enabled him to track John's whereabouts.

"Nothing gets by me but the wind," he'd tell his sons, and they knew that he was more often right than wrong.

McIntyre saw through his son's cover story. He asked if John was in some kind of money trouble and offered to help him out. He feared that John, looking for some fast cash, was resuming his fish-poaching antics.

John tried to reassure his father this time he really was just going out fishing with nets like everyone else. He explained that he simply didn't want Clayton and his friends to know that he had gone without them.

The old spook wasn't fooled by this yarn. Soon after John left, John senior got into his old Cadillac and followed him to the moonlit Gloucester pier. McIntyre counted two others boarding the *Valhalla* along with John: Anderson, and Sean. It seemed like a small crew for such a large fishing boat.

One hour after midnight on September 14, 1984, the *Valhalla* slipped out of Gloucester Harbor, past the Coast Guard station, and headed east across the blustery Atlantic to the Irish coast.

7

DOUBLE GAME

Clayton called the McIntyres' home at least once a day during the last half of September. No matter what excuse John's mother Emily offered for John's absence, he never tired of phoning.

Clayton was not so much concerned about John as he was angry. After the diabetic ulcer on his leg had healed, he had returned to the *Surge* to pick up his welding machine and rigging tools. The boat, however, appeared to be abandoned, and his tools had disappeared. And now so had John.

Having tired of Emily's excuses, he called Brendan Kelly, hoping for some news.

"I don't have anything more to do with the *Surge*," Brendan answered unhelpfully. About John he knew nothing.

Clayton continued to phone the McIntyres, but his calls became less frequent after the first couple of weeks. Clayton passed the time doing odd jobs for Walton and hanging around the Boston waterfront.

On one of his trips to Fish Pier, Clayton ran into Joe Murray. Joe told him where he could find his tools but said that he hadn't seen John around for several weeks.

*   *   *

133

Clayton Smith wasn't the only one interested in John Mc-
Intyre's whereabouts. Philip Brady was a career customs
grunt. Almost fifty, he walked with a slouch gained from a
lifetime as a plodding, old-fashioned investigator. His energy
and ambition had long ago lapsed into a dogged, unimaginative pursuit of the drug barons and petty hoods whose files
came across his desk.

Brady was one of the low men on the Federal Drug Task
Force team pursuing Joe Murray. He had first heard of John
McIntyre the previous January, when passport control at Logan informed him of John's departure with Murray for Amsterdam. Brady had no idea of the purpose of the journey. As
far as he was concerned, the trip was important only because
it was a violation of a court-ordered probation restriction on
international travel imposed after one of John's poaching escapades. At the time, Brady considered this infraction insuffi-
cient to warrant John's immediate arrest, but it was something
to keep in the files.

When customs was notified of Joe Murray's September
departure for Ireland, Brady decided to pay John a visit. It was
probably a waste of time, but Brady was used to pursuing
leads that went nowhere.

Brady went to Robbi's Quincy apartment, the only address he had. Robbi did as John had told her. She said only
that he was off with some friends and that he had been for
some time. On the day he left, John had offered Robbi no
details beyond the cover story about swordfishing, but she
knew that her Viking prince was embarking on a special
voyage. John's excitement and air of anticipation had been
apparent for weeks. This trip was evidently not a simple
fishing expedition. Robbi suspected that John's seafaring adventure had more to do with Ireland's northern counties than
Georges Bank.

Brady had no reason to doubt her story. But he had a
request of his own.

Robbi was an easy mark. She feared the law in a way that John never did. Brady left his card and told her to give him a call when John showed up. It would be for his own good, and hers, if she did as she was told, Brady said. Robbi nodded in agreement.

Pat Nee was getting nervous. It was September 29, three long days after the *Marita Ann* had set out for the rendezvous, and he still had not heard a word. Joe and his sick wife had left for Boston. Nee found himself sitting in a Dublin hotel, waiting for a phone call that might never come. He didn't know what to do next.

"Listen to the radio!" shouted his girlfriend, who, together with another couple had stayed in Ireland after the Murrays' unexpected departure. She turned up the volume.

Nee listened incredulously as the announcer reported the seizure of the *Marita Ann*." A tip-off from the United States has led to the arrest of five alleged IRA gunrunners and the seizure of more than five tons of machine guns, rifles, and ammunition aboard an Irish trawler," reported the radio announcer. "The arms had been transferred to the trawler from a larger ship in international waters off the southwest coast. A search is continuing for the other ship, which is thought to have loaded its cargo in the United States."

Nee grimaced as he turned away from the radio. His face was drained of all color; he looked as though he had been shot. Nee wasn't the type to stay calm in the face of such a calamity. All he knew was that he and his friends had to get out of Ireland fast.

Nee made a hurried call to Joe Murray in Charlestown. Their discussion was businesslike and to the point. Nee wanted four tickets waiting for them in Paris. Murray promised to make the arrangements. That day, Joe reserved four seats on TWA's October 2 flight from Paris to Boston at a local travel agency. The agent entered the names of Nee and his party as well as Joe's name and address in the computer.

Within hours of the announcement of the *Marita Ann*'s capture, Nee and the others were on a ferry across the Irish Sea to Holyhead, where they caught a connecting train to London's Paddington Station. Nee would have preferred to fly out of Heathrow on the short hop to Paris, but he feared the airport's notoriously strict passport control. Instead, they boarded the Paris train at Victoria and crossed the Channel by boat.

Two arduous days after deserting Dublin. Nee checked into a Paris hotel. Late that evening, he made a collect call to Murray's home to finalize details of his return trip. Joe then drove to the TWA terminal at Logan Airport to purchase the four Paris-to-Boston tickets he'd reserved earlier.

The agent suggested that the tickets could be purchased more cheaply in Paris because of the dollar's favorable exchange rate.

"I don't care," said Joe curtly. "I want to do it this way."

He paid the $1,740 bill in tens and twenties.

"Did you hit the number, or are you the bookie?" remarked the agent when she saw the bills.

Joe didn't answer. He walked over to a pay phone and made a final call to Nee at his Paris hotel.

Donald DeFago was waiting for Nee when he arrived in Boston at 2:40 P.M. on October 2. DeFago was a special agent with the U.S. Customs Service and a member of the Federal Drug Task Force stalking Joe Murray. He was young and ambitious, already more senior than Phil Brady and anxious to show his opposites in the DEA and the FBI that, contrary to popular belief, all customs agents were not bimbos.

A court-authorized tap on Joe Murray's phone had picked up his call to Nee in Paris. Both Nee and his traveling companion Jon Murray, a drug associate of Joe's, were on the watch list, and TWA had notified DeFago of their impending arrival.

Customs figured something was up, but they had no idea what it might be. DeFago, like his junior partner Brady, was interested in Nee and Murray as drug suspects. Although the *Marita Ann* had been captured three days earlier, he knew nothing about the *Valhalla* and its illegal arms smuggling.

DeFago told the inspectors manning the green and red customs lines at Logan to look carefully for any evidence of drugs in Nee's luggage and on his person but to conduct their search without arousing Nee's suspicions. He didn't want to alert Nee to the fact that he had been targeted.

The airport inspectors, however, were on their home turf. All DeFago could do was watch nervously while Nee and his companions were treated to a special pat-down search, which turned up nothing.

On the morning of October 3, Special Agent Steve Crogan at Boston customs received a telex from the U. S. embassy in London informing him of the *Valhalla*'s participation in the intercepted arms transfer. The British kept their sources to themselves but had alerted the DEA attaché in London that the *Valhalla* might be heading for a northeastern port.

Crogan much preferred drug investigations to gun-smuggling cases. He was a savvy bureaucrat and knew that the top man in the U. S. Customs Service, the media-hungry political appointee William von Raab, was anxious to make his mark as a leader in President Reagan's war against drugs. Drug cases were also comparatively easy to prosecute. Besides, there hadn't been an arms-smuggling trial in Boston for more than a century. It was only too easy for Crogan to envision an IRA lawyer arguing before a "green" Boston jury, turning a case of gun running into a political show trial.

But arms smuggling, like drug importing, was nonetheless a customs offense, and a new file was opened. A joint customs–Coast Guard lookout was ordered to coordinate the capture of the *Valhalla*. The Coast Guard was put on alert along the entire New England coast; the harbor patrol in Gloucester was ordered to keep a special watch for the vessel's return. Now all customs had to do was wait for the return of the ship and its still-anonymous crew.

The teletype in DEA's Boston headquarters clattered out a photograph from the DEA attaché in London. An agent took the black and white reproduction off the machine and copied it for distribution up the chain of command.

The picture had been taken by British intelligence the previous January. It showed John McIntyre standing in front of a ship on the Amsterdam dock where the *Marita Ann* and the *Ramsland* were moored.

When John and Murray had arrived in Amsterdam, British intelligence had been waiting for them. The British, however, were too concerned that U. S. Customs had been penetrated by the IRA—not without reason, after the trial of New York's Emerald Society revealed customs's IRA links—to share with Washington any information about a pending arms shipment. Instead, they continued to monitor the situation and kept John's picture in their files for safekeeping.

When the *Marita Ann* was intercepted, the British pulled out John's picture. Here, they decided, was their Boston connection to the IRA.

DEA and customs were ostensibly on the same team, but that didn't mean they had to cooperate with each other. Every failure of customs to stem the tidal wave of drug imports was viewed by the DEA as an opportunity to claim the mantle of supremacy in the drug battle. Why should the DEA pass on information that would enable customs to intercept a drug shipment when they could let the stuff come in, bust it, and take all of the credit themselves?

DEA officers, of course, would never put this preference

on paper. It sounded much better to suggest only that it was better policy to trace the drugs to their source onshore—which just happened to be DEA's turf—than to arrest them on the waterfront, where all the glory belonged to customs. But to the battle-scarred veterans of interservice guerrilla warfare, forced into an uneasy collaboration, such diplomatic formulations barely concealed each agency's self-aggrandizing objectives.

A few days later, John returned to Boston aboard the *Valhalla*. The sun had almost set as the ship passed the old Civil War fortress on Georges Island, where John had roamed as a youth. To their left was Long Island, now connected by a causeway to Squantum, John's hometown. As they sailed by Fort Independence on Castle Island, John couldn't help thinking of the contrast between his failed effort to force Britain's withdrawal from Ireland and George Washington's successful bombardment of this very fortress—Britain's chief stronghold in colonial America.

The *Valhalla* passed the army-base pier, next to the fort, and slipped along the Boston side of Pier 7, where the last survivors of the city's fishing tradition—and the new generation of smugglers—still unload their daily catch. The pier is composed of asphalt-covered sunken barges, ten yards wide, connected by a series of ramps, which rise and fall with the tides. Pier 7 juts about three hundred feet into the harbor, across from the Eastern Airlines terminal at Logan Airport on the harbor's northern shore. Anderson settled the *Valhalla* alongside Pier 7's outermost dock, right under the nose of an unknowing Coast Guard and the somnambulent U. S. Customs Service. There wasn't a federal agent in sight.

After tying up the boat, John and the others made the long walk past the quiet trawlers and ice house and through the parking lot to Northern Avenue, where they scattered into the chill of the fall night.

"I can only stay a little while," John said breathlessly to his parents. He closed the door to the house on Ocean Street, dropped his sea bag in the front hall by the stairway, and went upstairs to take his first real shower in a month.

After putting on fresh clothes, John walked downstairs and into his parents' kitchen. His bearded face was bronzed by the winter sun. Despite the fact that he hadn't slept well for many days, he looked vibrant and refreshed. Emily liked what the ocean did for her son. This trip, she saw, had revived him. Emily had learned to worry less about John when he was at sea than when he was on land. Besides, during his absence she had been so busy dealing with the cardiologists caring for her husband that John was rarely in her thoughts. Until recently, John senior had managed to defy his doctor's pessimistic prognosis. Now, his heart condition was steadily worsening.

John didn't want to tell his parents about his predicament. The less they knew the better. he explained only that he was exhausted from having been at sea for a month, and anxious to see Robbi. Things between them had been going well before he left, and John hoped that he and Robbi could resume where they'd left off.

When John phoned to say he'd be over shortly, Robbi seemed startled. He asked her to pick him up, but she protested that she had just stepped out of the shower and didn't want John's parents seeing her with wet hair. John complained that he didn't want to ask his ailing father for a ride, but Robbi was adamant. John put down the phone angrily. It wasn't quite the reception he was hoping for.

After their initial shock over John's divorce, Emily and John senior had come to like Robbi. They were thankful for her ability to revive the happy, carefree spirit John had lost during his STRATCOM posting. Years ago John's parents blamed Robbi for the breakup of his brief marriage, and then for the pain their subsequently rocky relationship had caused their son. She preferred to stay out of the McIntyres' way unless absolutely necessary. Robbi called back moments after John hung up and told him to phone again just before he was about to leave for her apartment.

Emily, who had been sleeping on the couch, overheard both phone calls and was annoyed at Robbi. But her more immediate fears concerned her husband's health. Her husband was annoyed as well. It was cold and snowing. Emily strained to defuse the tension between her two men, to reassert a sense of domesticity in a difficult situation. Fidgety, she went to fetch the dirty laundry in John's sea bag.

"Don't touch the bag," said John firmly. He carried it himself down to the cellar where his survival suits and other marine gear were stored.

John made a quick call to Robbi and told her his father was leaving to drive him to her apartment, less than a half-hour away. As they were going out the door, Emily put on her coat and came along as well. On the ride over, John hardly said a word, and his parents didn't press him. John senior was growing concerned about his son. He pulled into a variety store and bought John a six-pack, his way of making peace.

"Get some sleep son," the old spook said as John got out of the car. "We'll talk tomorrow."

On their way home, the McIntyres stopped to fix a broken wiper and saw a phalanx of Quincy police cars barreling past them in the opposite direction. John remarked to Emily that the guy they were after must really be loaded to deserve such a welcoming party.

John rang Robbi's bell, but no one answered. He went around to the backyard and climbed up the rear stairway to her second-floor apartment. He pounded on her door, but all remained quiet inside. He shouted for her but was answered with silence.

Robbi had disappeared. In her absence, she had arranged for someone else to greet her Viking hero. A posse of swirling blue lights filled the street below.

John knew at once that Robbi had informed on him. She'd called the police as soon as she had hung up the phone on her lover.

The cops dragged John off, kicking him hard as they stuffed him into the squad car. John was no stranger to the Quincy police, and they took advantage of their luck during the ride to the station. John was still gasping from the pain of their blows when he was thrown into a holding cell at the police station. One whole side of his body had turned black-and-blue from the beating.

"Hello McIntyre. My name is Philip Brady of the United States Customs Service. We've been waiting for you to get back."

Brady entered the cell only a few minutes after the door had closed on John. He knew that John had been out to sea for a number of weeks at the same time that the *Valhalla* was making its run to Ireland. And he had also pried away a copy of the photo in the DEA's possession, which appeared to connect John to the *Marita Ann*. Brady thought he had stumbled onto a gold mine.

The interception of the IRA shipment was big news. Brady saw himself at the center of a high-visibility investigation into international gun and drug smuggling. The sole lead—John McIntyre—belonged to him. Even a plodding grunt like Brady knew that this was an opportunity that might come once in a career. He was determined to make the best of it.

Early Sunday morning, Chris got a tip from the desk sergeant that John was being held at the station. Chris wanted to come down and bail his brother out, but his friend told him, "No way, Chris. This is bigger than both of us. You can't get near him."

John senior went to the police station despite this warning. He was an honorary chief of police, and everyone at the station knew him. This time, the cops couldn't help him.

"It's too big," the police said apologetically. "The Feds are involved." John senior turned to Emily and asked what in God's name was going on. The police were acting as if John were Al Capone.

They refused to consider a bail bondsman or to let John see a lawyer. John was floating between local and federal jurisdictions. His civil rights be damned, the Feds were holding on to John McIntyre until they were finished with him.

From the time John was picked up Saturday evening until the early morning hours of Sunday, Brady pressed him for hard information about his actions during the previous weeks.

John didn't think much of Brady. Despite his lack of sleep, he had no trouble deflecting his inquiries. Phil Brady was just as tenacious. He kept coming after John all through the night. "OK," said Brady, "tell us again where you were."

John repeated his cover story. He had been away partying on the Cape with friends. They had gone out fishing and gotten drunk. Nothing unusual in that, was there? John offered no names. He didn't know where his drinking buddies lived. They were just guys he had run into on the docks.

Could anyone vouch for his whereabouts? asked Brady. No, replied John, and he told his story yet again.

Brady never tired of listening to John's monologue. He was content to let him exhaust himself before he really got down to business.

It was hours before Brady let drop the first reference to the *Valhalla*. Customs, he said, knew that John was aboard the *Valhalla*. They even had a picture.

John wasn't surprised by this revelation but was familiar

enough with the Nimrod's capabilities to know that Brady had no pictures tying him to the ship. John had taken every precaution to keep his face out of view. Brady, he quickly decided, was bluffing.

"I don't know what you're talking about," answered John.

Brady smiled easily. "You're never heard of the *Valhalla*?" he asked.

"Sure," John answered. He had helped refit the ship a few months earlier. But that was all he did. Ask anyone around the docks, he protested. He was simply a disabled vet who picked up beer money doing welding and general repairs on the waterfront.

The regulars at the police station knew John from his poaching days. They warned Brady that John was a master at playing the wronged innocent.

"He's full of it," said one cop simply.

Brady told them not to worry. He had this kid just where he wanted him. Turning to John suddenly, he asked, "Where is the *Valhalla*?"

"Last time I saw her was up in Gloucester," answered John sharply and as coolly as he could. "I was hired to do a rush job for some company called Leeward Inc. I got paid off and I left to go party."

John couldn't believe it. Customs had him, but they had yet to find the *Valhalla*. Brady, he decided, was a buffoon. In his wildest dreams he had never believed that the ship would remain undetected. And if Brady had found him before he found the *Valhalla*, it confirmed John's suspicion that Robbi had given him up to the Feds.

"You're not going anywhere until you tell us where she is," announced Brady abruptly. He was beginning to believe John's protestations. Brady lacked hard evidence linking John to the arms smuggling, and his story, though not unchallengeable, made sense. Brady's only solid lead was DEA's photo—and he was saving that for later.

Double Game

John's first interrogation was over. He was left alone for a few hours' sleep.

After some sleep and a quick breakfast early Sunday morning, Brady returned to the Quincy police station. John was brought into a small room, empty except for a wooden table and chairs. Brady's questions revealed a new direction to the inquiry. He explained that customs wasn't after John, who he admitted was just a cog in the machine run by Joe Murray. Murray was the one they were after. Brady said that customs knew Murray was in the IRA. But didn't John know that Joe was just milking his connection with the Provos in order to line his own pockets? Murray had been working for the Mob for years, running everything from cocaine to counterfeit bills. Didn't John know?

John was only too aware of Joe's double-dealing. But he was surprised to discover that what he had only reluctantly admitted to himself was common knowledge among the paper-pushers working for customs.

"I don't know anything about the IRA," said John unconvincingly.

"Then what were you doing on the *Marita Ann* in Amsterdam?" asked Brady, tossing the DEA photo across the table and over to him.

John felt the heat rising in his face as he looked at the picture. It showed him standing on the pier in Amsterdam, with the looming hulk of a ship in the background. He couldn't believe his eyes. He had been under surveillance since January! The whole operation had been over before it had even begun, strangled in its infancy by an informer. John's suspicions turned yet again to Joe Murray.

John took a closer look at the picture. Very calmly he asked, "What's this supposed to be?"

Brady stated that the picture tied John conclusively to the

Marita Ann, the weapons-carrying trawler that had been seized a couple of weeks earlier.

John looked honestly puzzled, just as the Quincy cops had warned. He claimed ignorance of the *Marita Ann* and casually dropped the observation that the boat in the picture was far too large for a trawler.

John had realized, after his sudden shock passed, that Brady had a picture of John coming off the *Ramsland*, not the *Marita Ann*. Customs evidently couldn't tell the difference between an ocean-going freighter and a little fishing trawler!

The atmosphere in the room changed perceptibly. Only moments earlier, John had been feeling the pressure of the investigation. Customs's stupidity, however, had created an entirely new situation. Power in the room had flowed away from the Feds. Brady had played what he thought was an ace, only to have it come up a joker. DEA had fed him the wrong information, making him look like a fool in the eyes of his only lead. Brady had committed a major error, squandering whatever respect John may have had for him. And he might never win it back.

Brady was no poker face, and his blank, disconcerted expression betrayed his loss. He announced brusquely that John would be held on a probation violation of a previous district-court offense. Brady had evidence that he had traveled to Amsterdam, a clear breach of his probation. He would be arraigned the following day. In the meantime, John could sit in his cell and ponder his options.

John was feeling confident. He had effortlessly refuted the evidence Brady possessed and would soon be out on bail. But his probation violation might very well mean a prison term.

John could not abide the thought of being caged in a cell. Just weeks before his army court-martial sentence was scheduled to end, he had broken out of the stockade for no better reason than his loathing of involuntary confinement. He was determined never to let it happen again, no matter how short the sentence.

Perhaps he could use Brady to stay out of prison and to frustrate customs's investigation as well. John had seen Brady in action. He was certain he could play the inquiry his way and make good on the promise he had made to himself during the *Valhalla*'s troubled voyage home.

John no longer felt any obligation to protect Joe Murray from his own greed and stupidity. His only concern was to salvage what might remain of the Boston IRA and to refashion it for a propaganda offensive against the British occupation. On both counts, Joe Murray was expendable.

Brady was getting up to leave when John unexpectedly announced that he was thinking about cooperating.

Brady's sullenness disappeared immediately. John was encouraged by this reaction. Brady all but stood at attention, so anxious was he to hear what John was about to say.

John admitted that he had traveled to Amsterdam, but not for anything to do with the IRA or the *Marita Ann*, about which he knew nothing. Brady's picture, he explained, showed him in front of the *Ramsland*—a drug freighter belonging to the Mob. Murray had sent him to look over the vessel and do some welding. He had been told the ship was going to be used for drug smuggling, but he didn't ask any questions as long as he got paid.

If Brady would keep him out of jail, John suggested innocently, perhaps he could find out more about the operation.

In his excitement, Brady saw "confidential source" written all over John. Brady was now convinced that John had not been aboard the *Valhalla* for the arms transfer. His information about this other ship might give customs something solid on Joe Murray.

Brady quickly offered John a deal. He guaranteed that if John cooperated with customs's investigation of Joe Murray, his problems with the Quincy court would be finessed. John would be arraigned as scheduled the next morning for his parole violation, but sentencing would be delayed for a couple of months—enough time for John to make good on his part of the bargain.

John had just made an impulsive decision that could put him in great danger. But at the time, he had to summon all of his strength just to keep from laughing aloud. He could only think about how he would give Brady the *Ramsland*, whose identity even the Feds would no doubt eventually discover. He told himself that he would never betray the IRA, despite what he suspected Joe Murray had done.

Robert Scott managed Pier 7, and like any manager worth his salary, Scott knew when he saw the *Valhalla* first thing Monday morning that something was out of place. He hadn't given permission for the ship to dock, so he boarded her to investigate.

Scott, a former commercial fisherman, knew a drug boat when he saw one. The rusted winches and pulleys aboard the *Valhalla* raised his suspicions, as did the vacuum cleaner he spotted in the *Valhalla*'s wheelhouse. Fishermen have no use for the contraptions, but drug runners often use them to clean up the decks after off-loading drugs.

Scott put in a call to the Coast Guard's safety officer and supplied him with the *Valhalla*'s name and registration number. Two Coast Guard officers showed up at Pier 7 later that day. According to a subsequent customs report, the two men, whose service had ostensibly been put on full alert looking for the ship, "found nothing out of the ordinary wrong about the fishing vessel and departed Pier 7."

At about the same time as Bob Scott was informing the Coast Guard that the *Valhalla* was docked along Pier 7, customs agents were driving John McIntyre to his parents' home. He had been held incommunicado for thirty-six hours;

denied not only sleep but even the most elementary legal protection, including the customary phone call.

John senior helped his son into a chair. John pulled up his shirt and displayed the angry black-and-blue bruises where he had been beaten by the zealous cops.

"I'm in deep trouble and I just came to warn you," John said abruptly. For the next hour, he spilled pieces of his *Valhalla* adventure to his astonished parents. He was confident that the Nimrod photos would not be clear enough to identify him. He insisted that when the *Valhalla* was discovered at Pier 7, the Feds wouldn't have a clue as to the identities of its crew.

The only problem, John suggested, was that Sean might have been wearing John senior's military intelligence cap when he was captured.

His father exploded. He had listened incredulously to his son's fantastic tale; it only confirmed his opinion of the IRA as a bunch of empty-headed bunglers. From what he could determine, his son had much more to worry about than an incriminating hat. But this example of amateurism gave the police a direct line to him.

"Jesus Christ," he bristled. "Don't you think the British have Sean in custody now? The first thing they are going to ask him is where he got that hat. No matter what he tells them, they're going to think your family was involved. What have you done?"

Involving one's family in intelligence operations was a cardinal sin. At no time during John senior's border-crossing days were Emily or John junior ever in any danger. And when his cover had been blown, it was only a matter of hours before he had them spirited out of Europe, beyond the reach of the KGB.

John, in contrast, had left the British what amounted to a calling card from John McIntyre, Sr. Escaping from the KGB was one thing. Hiding from American investigators was something else indeed.

John could only reply that Sean wouldn't be so stupid as to hold onto the hat. No doubt, he said, Sean had thrown it overboard before the *Marita Ann* was captured.

His father wasn't so sure. John looked like he was ready to collapse, but didn't want his parents to worry.

"I'm all right," he said. "I just want to get some sleep."

As they watched John walk up the stairs to his old bedroom, John's father said that someone by the name of Joe had been calling repeatedly.

"He says it's urgent. Something about the boat."

John had neither the energy nor the desire to speak with Murray. Joe called several more times that Monday and again on Tuesday morning. John refused to talk to him.

Tuesday morning, after his first sound sleep in weeks, John explained to his parents about Joe Murray's role in his predicament. He told his father about Joe's failure to command the *Marita Ann* and about the existence of an informer who had compromised the operation even before John had visited Amsterdam the previous winter.

"Joe Murray could very well have realized that he himself gave the story away to people in Ireland," speculated John. "Maybe that's why he returned to Boston rather than take the *Marita Ann* out with the crew."

The former master spook told his son that in his experience cowards were more common than traitors.

"Let's see if he even made it to Ireland," said John senior. He picked up the phone and called one of his many friends still active in law enforcement. A few minutes later, his source phoned back. The computer system at Logan Airport confirmed that Joe Murray had definitely flown to Ireland.

The next time Joe called, John agreed to speak to him.

Joe told John that the Feds had still not located the *Valhalla*. John couldn't help thinking that it was Joe's Coast

Double Game

Guard supersource rather than gross incompetence that had kept Brady and the others away from the boat for four long days.

John wanted to sail the *Valhalla* out of Boston Harbor and scuttle her at sea. But Murray was more concerned about losing the quarter-million–dollar boat. He ordered John to return to the *Valhalla* and destroy any incriminating evidence.

"Only if you come in person," demanded John coldly.

"Yeah, see you in one hour."

Whatever John's suspicions about Joe, he was still the top man in the Boston IRA and, John had to admit, someone who had been a close friend once. It wasn't easy for John to keep these natural sympathies from clashing with a more rational judgment of Joe's culpability. Had John suspected anyone but Joe of treachery, he never would have been so generous.

"Screwing around with John McIntyre was the worst thing you could ever do. But Joe was still the boss, and John gave him the benefit of the doubt. He wouldn't have given anyone else a second chance," Chris later recalled.

After speaking with Murray, John went down to the cellar where he had stowed his sea bag. When he opened it, his Luger and 9mm pistols were still inside. But along with his dirty laundry, Emily had taken the dark blue logbook detailing the *Valhalla*'s voyage.

John bolted up the stairs in a rage. If that logbook fell into the wrong hands, the Feds would have a blueprint of the entire operation.

John sat Emily down on the living-room couch, put his hands on her shoulders, and, as calmly as he could, asked her to give him the log. But Emily was so disconcerted by John's fury that she temporarily forgot where in the cellar she had put it.

John ran downstairs and began tearing the cellar apart. He soon found the book, shoved it into a brown paper bag, and walked out the front door.

John senior drove John into Boston and dropped him off one block from Pier 7. As John approached the *Valhalla*, he spotted Anderson, Murray, and Pat Nee.

"Where the hell were you?" John demanded. Friend or no friend, John wanted some quick answers to questions that had dogged him for weeks.

"My wife was sick," shot back Murray, whose crimson face betrayed his embarrassment. "I had to fly her home right away."

"Your wife was sick!" exclaimed John, incredulous. It was such a lame explanation, thought John, it might be true. Perhaps his father was right. But he knew that if he had been in Murray's place, nothing would have kept him from his obligation to command the *Marita Ann*.

Murray had learned of John's arrest, but John explained that he had only been picked up on a parole violation. Neither he nor Anderson mentioned anything about the incriminating photos taken by the Nimrod; John kept quiet about the Amsterdam snap shot that Brady possessed.

"They have nothing on us if we get the prints off the boat. They've got nothing on us," Joe repeated. "They've got a boat and that's all."

John and Anderson started towards the gangplank. There was plenty of work to do aboard the *Valhalla*.

"Aren't you going to help, Joe?" John asked quietly.

Murray wasn't planning to stay a moment longer than necessary. He had to leave immediately, he announced, and thrust a paper bag into John's hand.

"Here's ten grand. Take it," he said sharply, as he walked away from the boat with Nee. Once again, John watched silently as Joe, his benefactor and commanding officer, turned his back and ran.

"Fingerprints first," said John to Anderson once they were aboard. "We may not have much time."

For the next three hours John and Anderson wiped down

the *Valhalla*, destroying whatever incriminating evidence they could find.

Joe Murray should never have visited the *Valhalla*. He led the astonished DEA agents of the Federal Drug Task Force directly to the boat. They followed Murray to the pier and observed his delivering the brown bag to John. But they didn't reveal their presence immediately. First, there were important arrangements to make. This DEA bust would be choreographed to humiliate customs. Not only had Brady and De-Fago been unable to locate the *Valhalla*, but Brady had let John McIntyre walk out of Quincy jail a free man only the day before. The local television news station had to be alerted. What good was a bust, after all, if it couldn't be seen in the eleven o'clock news?

Unfortunately for the DEA, Robert Scott, the stubborn manager of Pier 7, was a man who refused to take no for an answer. After being rebuffed on Monday by the Coast Guard, Scott had called customs on Tuesday morning to repeat his suspicions about the *Valhalla*. Customs agents arrived at the pier just as the film crew alerted by the DEA was unloading its gear. Federal agents from competing bureaucracies were stumbling all over each other in their efforts to grab the glory for the *Valhalla*'s capture. In their enthusiasm, however, one important detail had been overlooked. No one had thought to get a warrant to board the ship.

Anderson was below flushing paper down the head as the Feds made their way up the gangplank. John got a quick hold on his wits and barred the way onto the deck.

"This is a documented vessel," he announced. "You cannot board this vessel without a maritime warrant. If you try, I have the legal right to shoot you."

John was right, and the embarrassed Feds knew it. They couldn't make an illegal seizure, especially in front of the cameras, which whirred on as the Feds scurried to get their paperwork in order. John stood calmly by the gangway, listening to the reassuring flush of Anderson at work.

If John was going to insist that the Feds observe the letter of the law, they were ready to oblige. Customs agents returned with not only the maritime warrant, but also with regulation manacles and leg irons. The television crews recorded John being led off the *Valhalla* in shackles by a U. S. marshal.

In their preliminary search of the *Valhalla*, agents discovered marine charts and John's handwritten notations of longitude and latitude systematically recorded on a calendar during a seventeen-day period beginning with the *Valhalla*'s departure on September 14. The charts were suitable only for navigation to the Flemish Cap, a fishing area east of Georges Bank off the Newfoundland coast. But John's informal register placed the *Valhalla* at the rendezvous area off the Irish coast.

John and Anderson were bundled into a car and taken to the customs offices in the JFK office complex at Government Center. As they were being hustled into the offices, John whispered to one of his guards that he wanted to speak privately with Brady. Anderson was quickly taken off in another direction, and John was put into a separate room to wait for Brady.

Brady didn't like being taken for a fool. Customs, despite its advance knowledge, hadn't been able to find the *Valhalla* for days, even as it sat barely a mile from its downtown offices. And Brady himself had just filed a written report clearing John of any knowledge of the *Valhalla*'s involvement in arms smuggling. Yet the next day, John was on the evening news being led off the very same ship.

Embarrassment was only part of Brady's problem. DEA was also moving onto Brady's turf. Its agents, based upon the photo telexed from their offices in London and today's discovery on Pier 7, had listed John as *their* source.

John did some quick thinking while he waited for Brady. He realized that his meeting with Joe Murray had been a major mistake. The Feds could not connect Joe to the *Valhalla*, and John was beginning to look like a key player in Joe's affairs.

When Brady walked in, John was ready. Was Brady trying to get him killed? he asked angrily. John explained that he knew Brady wanted drug information. He was trying to keep his part of the bargain struck in the Quincy police station. That's why when Murray called him that morning and offered him some easy money to clean out the *Valhalla*, he agreed to meet him.

A quick "bullshit" was all that Brady could manage. John's explanation had put him off balance.

John insisted that customs check the phone records; they would prove that Murray had called him. In fact, John continued when the Keystone Kops had stormed the *Valhalla*, he had been pumping Anderson for information about Murray's next job.

"So what did you find out?" Brady asked skeptically.

"I found out about the *Ramsland*," replied John. "Murray plans to bring a freighter of dope right into Boston."

Brady fidgeted nervously. The DEA was on his heels. He had already been embarrassed once by John. If he was taken in again, he'd be a laughingstock—and with good reason.

Brady called for a stenographer to take a statement. John was a risk, but one worth taking. The revelation about the *Ramsland* and its impending drug haul had already provided Brady with enough ammunition to silence the DEA. For the first time, customs would have advance, inside information on one of Joe Murray's operations. The *Ramsland* bust would break his gang wide open and give the Feds enough hard evidence, at last, to put Murray himself behind bars. Brady could now look his antagonists straight in the eye and complain that their prime-time bust aboard the *Valhalla* had endangered his investigation. Brady had walked into the biggest opportunity of his career. John, he decided, was a promotion ticket to be sure.

John quickly established his own ground rules for his cooperation. He knew that if his name was placed in customs's paper mill, he was as good as dead. He told Brady that he would deal exclusively with him and would make no written statements and take no money. He would provide information only and would not testify against anyone. But he would help them bust the *Ramsland.*

Brady agreed to these conditions. He assumed that John was worried about the DEA, but it was Murray's IRA mole in the Coast Guard that he feared.

Brady excitedly briefed his superiors on his new confidential source. The *Ramsland* sting would be handled exclusively by customs. The other, more senior agents, were visibly distressed by Brady's coup. Professional jealousy was part of it. They also suspected that he had been conned.

While Brady was singing John's praises, John and Anderson were being freed. As John walked out of the JFK complex, one of the agents called out, "If we ever find that you were on the *Valhalla,* we'll break your back."

"Like I told you," said John breezily, "I'm just a welder."

John had a right to be in good spirits. Barely hours after he had been lead off the *Valhalla* in manacles, he was a free man. And he had convinced Brady of his sincerity and created an alibi for the mounting evidence against him.

While John was being driven to the McIntyre's house, Chris and his parents were watching his televised arrest aboard the *Valhalla.* Chris didn't anger easily, but he was concerned for his parents and the effect John's escapades would have on his father's failing health. The last thing he needed was to endure the pain and public humiliation of exhibitions like the one they had just seen at Pier 7.

That evening when John walked through the front door of his parents' house, smiling at his good fortune, Chris snapped. He had never bested John in a fight, but his rage overwhelmed him. He and John went at each other in the cellar. Emily called the police to end the brawl, but even the police had difficulty stopping Chris, who pummeled the cops before they eventually subdued him. The McIntyre boys were battered and bruised and ever more oppressed by the consequences of John's zeal.

His father could not understand why his son became involved in the IRA. "Look, I'm not apologizing for anything," retorted John in anger. "I joined the IRA because I believe in it. Those people in Ireland don't have anything. They are being crushed in their own country. You and Ma always used to quote Saint Thomas Aquinas. Well, you know what he says about revolution? 'If all else fails, people have a right to use violence as a last resort to bring about the end of an unjust ruler.'

"I don't agree with some of their tactics, and I don't like some of their people," John admitted. "But their cause is just, and they need me. Maybe in time," he added earnestly, "I can convince them that they can't beat the British with bullets. The IRA has to get the governments of the free world to intervene. The Irish people can't do it alone. I will fight with them no matter what happens. If it means playing a trick on the Feds, so be it."

John's heartfelt enthusiasm made John senior fear more than ever for his son's safety. An unhealthy desire for martyrdom was getting the better of him. His father wondered how his son could think he would outwit his pursuers on the federal task force, not to mention his so-called friends— mobsters and revolutionaries alike. Had he himself carried as much emotional baggage around with him during his cold-war exploits, John's father thought, he wouldn't have lasted more than a few weeks.

"You can't play tricks on these guys," he warned. "It kills you." John senior insisted that John's double game couldn't succeed. In his experience, double agents rarely survived their reckless intrigue. And he put little stock in Brady's promises of confidentiality, the key to John's survival. He knew from firsthand experience how easily a government agency could be infiltrated.

While the elder McIntyre agonized over his son's fate, John put the finishing touches on his master plan. If all went according to his blueprint, John would throw Brady the *Ramsland*—a marijuana bust that John figured would only result in the most lenient of jail sentences, if anyone went to jail at all. Even if Murray managed once again to walk away clean from the *Ramsland*, his days as head of the Boston IRA would be over. The leadership in Ireland could not overlook both the *Valhalla* fiasco and the loss of the *Ramsland*. John contemplated a fantastic opportunity to step in and shape the organization in his own image. Once Murray was out of the picture, John thought, security leaks and drug dealings would be a thing of the past. Public sympathy, not public scandal, would be the new IRA strategy under John McIntyre's leadership.

8

~~~~~~

THE *RAMSLAND*

"So," John's father asked, "what are you going to do about Robbi?"

John laughed and said that he was on his way over to her apartment.

"Are you nuts?" John senior exclaimed. "She set you up! She's the one who turned you in, and you're going to sleep with her?"

"Every night," replied John. The humor was gone from his voice. His face was now steeled and determined. "I'm going to do to her what she did to me."

Robbi was waiting nervously when John knocked on her door. She guessed that John suspected her and only hoped that he would accept the explanation she had devised during the last several days.

"Oh John," she said quickly. "It was all my fault. I had taken a sleeping pill before you called, and I just crashed. I didn't hear you knock or anything. That old biddy across the hall must have called the police. Are you OK? You look terrible. Do you want a beer? C'mon and sit down."

When Robbi was jittery, she tended to chatter.

John was not at all surprised by her performance. Like

159

her, he too had to make the lies he was about to speak seem like the truth.

"It wasn't you," he said reassuringly. "It was that asshole Murray. He was just using me. He even suckered me into going onto the *Valhalla* today."

"I know," she said. Robbi's pace had slowed considerably. "I saw the report on television tonight. How come you're out of jail?"

"I made a trade," he said dryly. "I'm going to work as a confidential source for the Feds."

"Oh Jesus, John, that's dangerous. Are you going to get paid?"

John could only marvel at Robbi's inability to camouflage her mercenary instincts. She was always quick to find her way to the heart of the matter, which for her invariably meant a payoff. John was hurt nonetheless. He loved this woman very much, but she had exposed him. For John, as for all the McIntyres, betrayal was the worst of all evils.

"You know," John replied, "I didn't think of that. They took ten thousand bucks off me this morning. They should give it back."

"They should give you more than that for what you're doing," she said indignantly.

Robbi's false solicitousness pained John like an open wound, but he was determined to exploit her greed for his own purposes.

It was much too dangerous for him to communicate directly with his contact at customs, he explained. Perhaps she could be his messenger to Brady and work out some payment for their services as well?

Robbi agreed enthusiastically, just as John had expected. As an intermediary, Robbi would be the protective layer between John and the Feds and would provide the assurance that Brady could never prosecute anyone on the information that

Robbi related directly to him; it was hearsay and could never be used in court.

John outlined the information Robbi was to give Brady. She could reveal the truth that he was on the *Valhalla* for its rendezvous with the *Marita Ann*—but only as a hired member of the repair crew. As for the *Ramsland*, all he knew was that it was scheduled to sail into Boston sometime in November.

During the next few weeks, Robbi and Brady conducted their business at little restaurants in out-of-the-way places on the South Shore. Brady was wowed by Robbi, who was used to charming men with her good looks. And Robbi wanted to please Brady. She told him about the *Valhalla*; when Brady pressed her for more, she supplied him with what she thought he wanted to hear—and would be willing to pay for. For the sake of Brady's cash, she admitted that John was one of the men who actually ferried the guns to Ireland.

She recalled a couple of names she had heard John mention and made them into members of the *Valhalla* crew. When Brady asked her about the paint chips imbedded in the gunnels of the *Marita Ann*, Robbi wrongly confirmed that the two boats had smashed together during the offloading at sea. Unwittingly, Robbi had actually helped John with this invention, as it sent the Feds on a fruitless investigation for a boat whose chips matched the ones they'd found. Fortunately, neither she nor the Feds ever realized that the *Valhalla's* dinghy was sitting openly on the *Marita Ann*.

Brady also wanted to know if there were any drugs aboard the *Valhalla*. Yes, Robbi volunteered, Murray was shipping cocaine to the IRA along with guns and light antitank weapons (LAWs) purchased on trips John spoke of Murray having made to Canada.

Robbi was spinning her own lies—investigators found no trace of cocaine or the LAWs on the *Marita Ann*—but Brady assumed that the information she passed came from John himself. John, it appeared, was proving to be an invaluable source, not only for the *Ramsland,* but also for the arms-exporting violations aboard the *Valhalla.*

Contrary to what John had hoped, the *Valhalla* investigation was moving quickly on a track entirely independent from the Federal Drug Task Force's pursuit of Joe Murray. Assistant U.S. Attorney Gary Crossen had convened a grand jury that had already begun hearing testimony. In a November 5 status report on the *Valhalla*/IRA investigation, Murray was described as the investigation's "main principal." A partial list of his summer weapons purchases had been compiled, and an upcoming examination of the captured weapons by FBI forensic specialists was expected to produce serial numbers and latent fingerprints implicating Murray, Nee, Anderson, and Crawley. Two days later, the first match was made between the serial numbers on one of Murray's gun purchases and a weapon seized on the *Marita Ann.*

In early November, John directed Robbi to tell Brady of an important upcoming meeting between him and Murray. On November 7, a surveillance team from customs followed John to Murray's home in Charlestown. Inside, John, Pat Nee, and Murray discussed the logistics of the *Ramsland*'s arrival in Boston Harbor.

Murray told John that the ship was carrying over thirty tons of marijuana hidden in the secret cargo hold John had ordered built during his stay in Amsterdam. It wasn't nearly as much as the *Ramsland* could transport, but it was enough for a test run.

Joe and John agreed on the following plan. John and a small crew would rendezvous with the *Ramsland* near Boston Light. They would board the 233-foot ship and trade places with the English crew, who would be whisked to Gloucester. John's crew would bring the *Ramsland* directly into the Boston army-base pier next to Pier 7. The army pier was ordinarily home to U.S. Navy ships requiring repairs and refitting.

The *Ramsland* was to be a phantom boat without paperwork or record of its entry into port. Murray's Coast Guard collaborator would have to ensure that no pilots went out to offer their services to guide the foreign vessel down President's Road and keep both the harbor master and customs officials from chancing upon the ship as she entered the harbor.

The initial docking at the army pier was merely a precaution. If for any reason the *Ramsland* was compromised, both John and Joe thought it better to save the Mob's shipyard, where the actual off-loading would take place, for a subsequent attempt.

After a few days at the army pier, the *Ramsland* would be towed to the Mob's shipyard, which offered repair facilities, dock space, limited access, and security. There, Murray had two choices. He could dismantle the old rusting hulk, a simple, nondescript salvage operation on a vessel that was a likely candidate for scrap. The marijuana would be removed as the salvage proceeded. Or he could use the *Ramsland* as a floating warehouse, sending it back for another run when her secret keel had been emptied. Just as the *Valhalla*'s run was envisioned as merely the inaugural arms shipment of the Boston IRA, so too was the *Ramsland*'s trip seen as the first of many megaton drug deliveries.

Robbi was instructed to tell Brady only that John had arranged to be a lumper on the crew that would sail out to meet the *Ramsland*. The ship was on its way to Boston, but John would not know until the day of the operation when the rendezvous was to occur. Brady should therefore make arrangements to follow the boat that would ferry John to the mother ship.

* * *

"Where did Dad go so early this morning all dolled up?" asked Chris. He and John were having breakfast at home on the morning of November 13.

"He went on a club trip to Connecticut with some of his retired army-intelligence friends," Emily replied. "They're going to hear a lecture tomorrow on intelligence and maritime security by an admiral in the Coast Guard."

The *Ramsland* operation had been set for that evening. If Brady discovered that John's father was having lunch with an admiral of the Coast Guard on the same day that Murray's Coast Guard source fixed the *Ramsland*'s passage through Boston Harbor to the army pier, he would naturally assume that John senior was the IRA's connection to the Coast Guard. And if Sean's hat was traced to its owner, the Feds would have one more piece of circumstantial evidence tying John senior to the IRA. John realized that by leading Brady to the *Ramsland* that day, he would not only seal Joe Murray's fate, he would implicate his father in the scheme as well.

John envisioned his father before a grand jury, faced with the grim prospect of lying or incriminating his son. John couldn't imagine a more bitter choice. He simply couldn't permit his father to be ensnared in problems that were of his own making.

John was losing control of the situation he thought he had mastered. He would have to wreck both Brady's and Murray's expectations for the *Ramsland* without either discovering his intention. John decided that instead of leading Brady to the *Ramsland*, he would chart a course that would take him away from the freighter. He could easily explain the mishap to Joe. Even if the bust was postponed for only one day, John could hope that it would be enough to keep his father out of Brady's calculations.

John left the table without finishing breakfast and headed for Walton's, where Clayton Smith still lived in a trailer. John and Clayton had reconciled after John's return in October. He had told Clayton about the arms-smuggling fiasco, declaring that his old friend was lucky to have been kept off the *Valhalla.*

John's knocking got Clayton out of bed. He explained that Murray had a job for them. A boat had to be sailed that day to Provincetown, at the tip of Cape Cod.

Clayton was not fooled by John. He knew that there was something else in the wind. Taking a boat to P-town was not the kind of job that would get John out on the road so early. Clayton still seemed resentful about being left off the *Valhalla,* although less so after John complained to him about what a difficult operation it had been. Now it looked like he would have his opportunity for adventure, whether he wanted it or not.

After buying some groceries for the trip, they went to the army-navy store in downtown Quincy to buy Clayton a coat to replace the one he'd forgotten in John's rush to leave Walton's. They were waiting outside when the store opened at eight. All the while, John stayed unusually close to Clayton. Clayton got the impression that John wanted to make sure he had no second thoughts about coming along.

After breakfast in a local diner, they drove past the capped sewer heads that had once spilled filth into the harbor and continued across the marsh to Marina Bay, a new condominium and recreational boat complex in Quincy. Customs agents assigned to Joe Murray watched John and Clayton greet Bob Anderson in the parking lot beside the grid of almost-empty docks. Joe Murray was waiting inside the Edmund Fitzgerald Restaurant, a tug turned restaurant moored at the far end of the boardwalk.

Murray was sitting alone in an oversized booth at one end of the restaurant, past the ornamental stairway, which led to the bar in the old wheelhouse upstairs, and rows of smaller, more intimate tables.

Joe had already briefed John privately on the rendezvous

and docking plan for the *Ramsland* that he had cleared with his collaborator in the Coast Guard. After meeting with the *Ramsland*, John, Anderson, and Clayton were to go aboard and trade places with the English crew on board. John would run the engine room, Anderson would navigate, and Clayton, the only mariner among them experienced in sailing vessels over eighty feet long, would pilot the ship into the army-base dock.

"Can you handle the job, Clayton?" asked Joe.

"You'll have to come in on the north side, because it's going to blow a gale of wind from the northwest," Clayton advised. "You can't go to work and take a strange vessel and come in against the wind to the dock. You have to get on the winded side and let her drift in. If you can get me a spring line ashore, and I want fast line handling, we can get that vessel in there with no problem at all."

Clayton was ready to do as he was told, but neither Murray nor John would tell him the first thing about the *Ramsland*. What kind of engines did this boat have? How many propellers? What kind of flag was she flying? Both Joe and John ignored his questions. Clayton was even kept in the dark about the *Ramsland*'s size.

What about the weather? Clayton continued. A gale was blowing from the northwest, he repeated, making for extremely rough water outside Boston Harbor.

Joe replied firmly that weather was not a factor in this operation. Clayton did not need to know that the Admiral had arranged everything for today. This was the first time he had been actually required to disrupt the Coast Guard's legal routine. Any postponement, Murry feared, would spook him.

Clayton was told that once he laid the ship beside the dock at the army base, his job was done.

"Is there any hot cargo on her?" he asked, only to be answered with blank stares. All Joe was interested in was the docking plan.

166

The *Ramsland*

Clayton asked about the vessel's registry, explaining that foreign boats couldn't simply enter an American port without flying the yellow quarantine flag.

"You don't go and bring a foreign ship in and just tie up on the dock. There is a procedure," he insisted.

No one was listening. Joe had fixed all of these concerns with the Coast Guard, but that part of the operation was none of Clayton's business.

John smiled and said, "Well, once you're in you don't get out." Clayton saw he had no choice but to do as he was ordered. All he had to do was dock the ship and keep his mouth shut. For that, he could expect a paper bag filled with twenty-five thousand dollars in ten- and twenty-dollar bills.

Clayton was in for yet another surprise. He assumed that the boat they would take to the rendezvous with the *Ramsland* in a winter gale would be some sort of large fishing boat. Instead, Clayton spotted the *Seven Winns*, a forty-footer, sailing its way up the channel to the marina.

"Here she comes!" someone cried.

The sailboat tacked around, and the skipper laid her port side up against the float. Clayton, John, and the others headed through the iron gates at the head of the main gangway leading down to the dock.

Clayton had no love for pleasure boats. As far as he was concerned, they only cluttered up the ocean. He feared that if they tried to tie this fiberglass pygmy alongside the steel-hulled *Ramsland*, she might very well sink. At the very least, she was going to be smashed all to pieces. Clayton was looking forward to being drowned.

Clayton complained loudly about the boat's equipment but was told to keep such concerns to himself. He boarded the sailboat along with John, Anderson, and Bill Winn. By the time they loaded everything on board and were ready to set out, the sky was darkening. As they cast off, John and Anderson watched Murray get into his car.

"What do you think?" John asked Anderson. They were both watching Murray speed out of the parking lot.

No reply was necessary. For both men, Murray's hurried exit stirred memories of their arrest one month earlier on the *Valhalla*. It was important to John's scheme to keep alive Anderson's lingering suspicions of a double cross.

As they cleared the inner harbor, heavy winds whipped the bitterly cold November air and rough seas. Could it be they were being set up once again? John wondered aloud. Anderson kept his eyes fixed on the radar screen, looking for the *Ramsland*—and for suspicious intruders as well.

Anderson's job was to direct the *Seven Winns* to the rendezvous northeast of Boston Harbor, off of Graves' Ledge. For hours, the *Seven Winns* bounced in the icy chop around a marker buoy. Down below, the crew took turns hiding from the weather. John was just able to tend the wheel from the aft cabin. His lower body stayed dry while his upper torso was beaten by the surf. Anderson watched the Loran radar and tried unsuccessfully to contact the *Ramsland* using a code known only to the freighter's captain.

Eventually, radio contact was established. Soon thereafter, the *Ramsland* appeared on Anderson's radar as well. But as the *Seven Winns* closed in on the *Ramsland*, so too did a mysterious blip on Anderson's radar screen.

"I think that's the Coast Guard out there," Anderson declared.

John encouraged him in his suspicions. "We want no part of this deal with the Coast Guard," he said. Anderson nodded affirmatively. "Let's get out of here."

He stuck his head down into the fo'c'sle and announced to those huddled below that he was taking the boat into Gloucester, a two-hour sail.

Anderson had indeed spotted the Coast Guard. Brady had

arranged for the cutter *Cape Morgan* to maintain surveillance on the *Seven Winns* and to locate the Ramsland. After fixing on the *Ramsland* by radar, the *Cape Morgan* followed it for several hours as it approached Boston Harbor, while at the same time maintaining a radar fix on the *Seven Winns.*

Around midnight, the commander of the *Cape Morgan* sighted both vessels as they neared their rendezvous. Some moments later, however, the *Seven Winns* made an abrupt turn away from the *Ramsland* and headed north instead.

It was close to two in the morning when the *Seven Winns* pulled into Brown's Boat Yard in Gloucester Harbor. The crew, minus Anderson, who went directly home, walked to the Dunkin Donuts shop nearby. From the pay phone outside, Bill Winn arranged for a couple of taxis to take them all back to the Quincy marina, where the day's journey had commenced some twelve hours earlier.

From John's standpoint, the stillborn rendezvous could not have gone better. He had successfully fanned Anderson's natural concerns, and the circumstantial connection to his dad had been severed. Both Brady and Murray would have to wait one more day for the *Ramsland* to enter Boston Harbor.

John, however, had neglected to consider what the *Ramsland*'s captain would do when the *Seven Winns* failed to arrive as scheduled.

The hapless *Ramsland*, tired of bobbing aimlessly in the icy winter seas, made its solitary way towards Boston in the early morning hours of November 14. The captain was unfamiliar with the harbor, and his unsteady course eventually attracted official attention. On two occasions, the Coast Guard asked the ship for its destination. After some hesitation, the captain replied that he was to dock at the army base in Boston Harbor.

A pilot was welcomed aboard at three in the morning on November 14. The captain didn't have enough cash on hand to pay for wharfage, nor could he name a local agent responsible for such charges, so the *Ramsland* was piloted to Anchorage 1 near Logan Airport.

That's when Brady and customs decided to move in. Brady knew something had gone wrong when the *Seven Winns* made for Gloucester without transferring John and the crew to the *Ramsland*. But experience had taught him that it was better to get part of the prize than to be greedy. Busting the *Ramsland* at its mooring might not reveal enough evidence to implicate Joe Murray, but it would tighten the noose customs was slowly closing around him.

Brady and his colleague DeFago also knew that it would only be a matter of hours before the *Ramsland* was boarded by harbor officials wondering why the vessel had so completely disregarded the standard procedures required for entering port. Better that customs get a share of the credit for intercepting the ship than cede all the applause to the Coast Guard.

DeFago himself boarded the *Ramsland* the next afternoon. He quickly discovered that the *Ramsland* had no papers, no country of registry. None of the crew was licensed, nor was the captain. A quick check of the DEA NADDIS computer showed that Scotland Yard had traced two of the crew to Las Palmas in the Canary Islands, where the *Ramsland* had picked up the cargo of marijuana earmarked for the United States.

Robbi had told Brady where the marijuana was hidden in the freighter, but customs preferred to disguise its foreknowledge. A narcotics-detecting dog was let loose on the ship. In the hold, it made the unlikely discovery of drugs hidden under tons of gravel in the false keel. By the afternoon of November 16, and many truckloads of gravel later, the first of thirty-three tons of marijuana bales was discovered.

Brady was angry that the seizure had not gone as planned, but the vessel and its cargo were headline news. And the Customs Service was riding at the head of the media parade.

The Ramsland

Murray was in a near panic. Joe had informed John of the ship's interception when John called to tell him of the postponement. He had been counting on the *Ramsland* to replenish his coffers and win back the good graces of the Mafia, which had been all but unable to ship marijuana into Boston since the *Hudson-D108* connection had been shut down nineteen months earlier.

Joe would have to explain the loss of both cargo and ship to a mobster whose organization was already under seige. The task force was closing in on Boston's entire organized-crime network. Patient investigators were working their way through the membership of the old Frankie LePere organization, which had been succeeded by Joe Murray's gang. Even Gennarro Angiulo, the head of the Boston Mob, had a bug in his house, which recorded intimate details of the New England Mafia and its operations.

At Heller's the next day, Clayton showed John an article in the *Boston Herald* announcing the *Ramsland* bust.

"Was that the ship we were supposed to take in?" Clayton asked.

"Yeah," John answered. They agreed how lucky they were that Anderson's intuition had been correct.

A few days after the *Ramsland* incident, Brady showed up in an out-of-the-way restaurant where John and Robbi were eating. He joined them and made a quick pitch to pay for John's assistance in another drug bust.

Brady and Gary Crossen had considered their options in the wake of their failure to tie Joe Murray to the *Ramsland*. The *Valhalla* investigation was developing some promising leads to Joe Murray, but if McIntyre could be convinced to work with them more closely—in a drug buy or, even better, as a court witness against Murray—there would be no question of Joe's conviction.

Customs needed John to take the stand against Joe Murray, Brady explained. If John agreed, Brady promised that he would be admitted into the Witness Protection Program and put forever beyond the reach of the Mob's retribution.

John stopped Brady before he detailed the offer. He refused to listen to such a risky scheme and told Brady to get lost. Brady was puzzled by John's brusqueness, but he left at once.

Brady was genuinely perplexed. After he left, Robbi explained to John that Brady had come at her suggestion. Customs was offering them big money—twenty thousand dollars—if John would work with them. Brady, she explained, wanted John to make a drug buy from one of Murray's lieutenants; Brady would then trace it back to Murray. Robbi simply thought that John should hear Brady's proposal for himself.

John never saw himself as an informer and therefore had no use for whatever enticement Brady offered. No matter what Joe Murray had done, John would never betray anyone for money. He considered the Witness Protection Program to be little better than a life-sentence of isolation and anonymity. Before his testimony, he would be kept under virtual house arrest at a secure federal installation, most probably a military base. After the trial, John McIntyre would cease to exist. Every agency of the federal government, from Social Security to the IRS, would conspire to create a new identity for him. He'd be forced to abandon his family and to surrender his dreams about resurrecting the IRA. It was too high a price to pay for the government's promise of safety.

Brady's offer simply didn't fit in with John's new game plan. He and some friends were going into business at the East Boston shipyard where the *Ramsland* was supposed to have been off-loaded. John had already bought one of Walton's cranes and transported it over to the yard. He planned to set up a legitimate ship-repair business that could fix anything that floated.

Customs, however, was not about to let John out of its

grip. Ever since their first meeting, John thought he had been playing Brady for a sucker, but customs had its own agenda—and was about to prove that it too could play hardball.

Brady had reported John's refusal to cooperate to the task force team at customs. He was content to maintain contact with John and to see whether Robbi could bring him around to cooperating, for cash, on another sting.

But Brady, like John, had completely misjudged the tenor of the investigation.

The British viewed the *Marita Ann* incident with unprecedented alarm, coming as it did on the heels of the IRA's incredible attempt on the lives of the entire British cabinet at the Grand Hotel in Brighton. The plans discovered on board the *Marita Ann* for a full-scale IRA military- and sabotage-training program supervised by Americans forced London to bring its case for vigorous American prosecution of the *Valhalla*'s IRA cadres directly to Washington.

On October 25, special agents from the customs offices in Boston and New York, together with the assistant U.S. Customs attaché in London, had been ordered to Washington for a special briefing of U.S. Customs Commissioner William von Raab and the U. S. ambassador to Great Britain, Charles Price.

Von Raab was a blustery political appointee almost universally scorned as ineffective by agents on the line, who had watched the flow of illegal drugs into the United States triple during his tenure. "Here is a man who is viewed by drug insiders and many congressional leaders as the mouse that roared," complained the head of the union representing customs employees. "Von Raab's expensive drug-fighting initiatives have included lots of hoopla, press parties, and glitz but little or no impact on beefing up interdiction where it is needed most."

Price was determined to provide London with hard information on the progress customs was making on their end of the *Valhalla* inquiry. Von Raab had summoned his minions to provide it.

The agents explained that they were slowly building on the evidence supplied by the Irish earlier that month. The paper trail on some of the weapons and military equipment was being unraveled, and agents were tracing physical evidence seized aboard the *Valhalla* as well.

The ambassador demanded something more tangible than this standard progress report. Von Raab wanted to please Price, whose connections reached directly into the Oval Office. He suggested that the two agents from Boston tell him about customs's confidential source.

The agents refused. The commissioner's request was an absolute breach of security. Brady would never forgive them if they compromised John's identity in any way.

Von Raab didn't like being embarrassed by his own men. He gave the agents a direct order to tell Price what they knew.

The agents swallowed their professional pride and reluctantly explained that they had developed a confidential source in the Boston IRA who refused to testify in public but who had been helpful both on the *Valhalla* case and on a forthcoming drug shipment.

"Tell them the name of the source," von Raab ordered.

The agents did as they were commanded, but insisted that the ambassador never relay John's name to the British. The agents knew, however, that Price could well decide to ingratiate himself with the British by revealing John's identity. Even if he didn't, it was now clear that both London and Washington would break all the rules in order to make their case against the Provos and the Boston IRA.

The agents returned to Boston determined to compel John to seek federal protection and thus save himself from almost certain retribution by the IRA. They grumbled to their colleagues about what they had been forced to divulge. But no one had the heart, or the courage, to tell Brady that his confidential source had been exposed.

When Brady reported his failure to win John's further cooperation, the two agents decided to implement their own freelance strategy to force his collaboration.

John was at Heller's, nursing a beer and musing over his fate when two men, obviously strangers to the place, walked through the door. John immediately recognized them as a couple of Brady's partners. Heller's was, as usual, thick with hard-drinking dockworkers.

Each man took a chair and sat down on either side of John.

"How ya doin, buddy," one said with exaggerated friendliness.

"Get the fuck out of here," replied John in a clenched whisper. "Are you trying to get me killed?"

The men smiled and left quickly.

John couldn't believe he was being double-crossed by grunts from Brady's office. It was obvious that customs, in its typically graceless fashion, was now trying to blackmail him. If he didn't cooperate in its investigation of Joe Murray, customs would expose him as an informer to his buddies in the IRA and the Mob. And John didn't have to imagine what his fate would be if Murray suspected that he had caused the gun-running fiasco. And not only that. Murray would never believe that John had sacrificed the *Ramsland* to draw attention away from the IRA and the *Valhalla*.

John came alone to his parents' house for Thanksgiving dinner. He arrived looking sad and beaten. The energy Emily had seen in his face the night he had come off the *Valhalla* had been drained by a month of constant intrigue and worry. John had begun to believe that his luck was running out.

Every few minutes, John walked over to the front window and glanced through the curtains.

"What is it, John?" asked his father.

John told him to take a look for himself. A dark-blue sedan was parked down the street on the side opposite their house.

"It's customs," John said. "They've been tailing me day and night for four weeks. They're being real obvious about it. Those bastards are trying to paint a bull's-eye on my back so big the IRA can't miss it."

"Please John," his father said, placing a reassuring hand on his son's shoulder, "tell me what's going on. All of it."

"What's the use?" John replied despondently. John had tried to emulate the wiliness of his father and the courage of his grandfather. The result, however, was a cruel parody of their achievements.

John poured out the story of his failed efforts to outsmart the Feds. Now, he said, they were pursuing him wherever he went. He wasn't certain, but he thought that Crogan, or DeFago, or his partner Chris Nelson had followed him into Heller's.

Word of John's contact with the Feds would soon get back to Murray, who would assume that John was under protective surveillance. He had already refused the Witness Protection Program, he told his father. But now customs was trying to drive him into it; he was being forced to choose between testifying against Joe Murray and the IRA or being killed by them. The U.S. government was holding a gun to his head and waiting for Murray to pull the trigger.

"Maybe you're imagining things," suggested his father with more hope then conviction. But the next day, his father saw the car again. So did Emily and Chris.

John senior stepped into the breach of fear and uncertainty. In his day, a promise from the U.S. government had been as solid a commitment as anyone could hope to receive. Even Nazis were protected because agents like McIntyre had assured them of Washington's reliability. What customs was now doing to his son reminded him more of the lemon squeeze reserved for the enemy. Their duplicity sickened him.

He told his son not to go to work or visit his usual haunts. He was to stay at his parents' house—for a week if necessary. If customs couldn't get to him, they couldn't play games with him. They would soon tire of the boredom and expense of a surveillance operation that wasn't producing.

John spent the next few days penned in at his parents' house, reading books from his father's library. Every evening he would sneak out to Robbi's through the back door, which led to the street at the far end of their yard, returning to Squantum before dawn. John was planning something for his avaricious lover and didn't want her becoming suspicious about his absence.

Just as his father predicted, the agents watching the house grew bored after a few days and disappeared. John began to believe that if he could only wait Brady out, he could get on with his life as though nothing had happened.

On the evening of Wednesday, November 27, the McIntyres were reading when they heard a tremendous crash on the front steps. Mr. McIntyre started at the noise, which sounded like something had been thrown against the aluminum storm door. He opened the door. At his feet lay Duke, the big white family cat, in the last stages of a convulsive death rattle. There was no evidence that John's pursuers had killed the animal, but John's situation did not allow for simple coincidences.

The next day, John helped his parents bury their beloved cat in the backyard. As they walked over to the garage to put the shovels away, John gestured in the direction of the street. The blue sedan had returned.

"It's no use," said John dejectedly, "They'll keep it up. They won't stop. They want me too bad."

Emily was forced to agree. In Pullach, she had learned that the Nazis had no monopoly on cruelty and corruption. Like her son John, she too had once believed in her power to redeem good from evil. Her husband had saved her from the dangerous folly of her freelance investigation into postwar U.S.–Nazi collaboration, but John had no one to rescue him from the consequences of his ill-considered enthusiasm. The new Nazis were after her child to spy for them. Such things weren't supposed to happen in America, Emily told herself, but the blue sedan outside their door could not be denied. John, she decided, had to escape, just as she and John senior had escaped thirty years earlier, before the web of betrayal had tightened around him.

John and Emily sat down on a couple of cinder blocks in the backyard. "You've got to get out of the country," she told him. "Make a new life somewhere: South America, Australia. The only way you can survive is to run fast and don't look back." It was the same creed that had protected her husband a generation earlier. Perhaps, Emily prayed, it would work for her son as well.

John agreed easily. He would not betray the IRA, whatever the personal cost. Escape seemed to promise a quick and honorable end to his torment.

Emily suggested that John flee to her relatives in Germany or drive across the border to Canada.

"I could drive you to Montreal," she offered.

"No, no," John replied. "Dad is very bad."

"John. Let us help you," Emily pleaded.

"It's OK, Mom," said John. "I'll be all right."

John had already caused his parents enough heartache. He would not permit them to involve themselves more deeply. No one would know how or to where he was escaping. His family could not be pressured into telling customs something they didn't know.

That night, John called Robbi to tell her he was ready to work with Brady. She was to arrange a meeting with him at half-past five the following evening at the Hollow Restaurant in Quincy.

"Have Brady bring the twenty thousand dollars and a written agreement," he said. "I'll set up another bust if they promise I won't have to testify against Murray."

Robbi was ecstatic. She would finally see the money Brady had dangled before her. And John had just told her she could have it all.

The deal he was offering wasn't everything that Brady wanted, thought John, but it was enough to keep him interested. As for Robbi, the promise of twenty thousand dollars cash would guarantee her presence that evening.

John, however, had no intention of carrying through with the bargain. Brady would arrive, bag of money in hand, and meet Robbi, who was so close to making her big score. John wouldn't be there to witness the scene, but he could imagine it—his sweet revenge for two who only wished him ill. By the time Brady and Robbi realized they had been duped, John planned to be safely at sea. He had already put his plan in motion.

Late Wednesday evening, he had arranged to meet Clayton at the huge East Boston dry dock next to the Metropolitan District Commission warehouse where Walton had stored his trucks.

John told Clayton that customs was squeezing him to testify against Murray, and he feared for his life if Murray found this out. He outlined his plan to escape offshore in one of his survival rafts and catch a freighter bound for Central or South America. Did Clayton know of any captains who would give him a ride?

The next morning, John got a phone call. His ocean ride

was all set for the following evening. Friday, November 30, would be John McIntyre's last day in America.

His monthly disability check from the VA arrived in Friday morning's mail. John was all but broke. Most of his savings had been spent buying Walton's tug and outfitting the *Valhalla*. John senior asked his son if he could use some extra cash; John was embarrased to accept his father's offer, but both Emily and John could see that their son was desperately short of money. John's father, habitually distrustful of banks, ferreted out a money belt and pulled three thousand dollars from its pouch. It wasn't much, but there wasn't enough time to do more.

"How will we know if you've made it away all right?" his distraught father asked. It would be too dangerous for John to contact his parents directly.

It was decided that as soon as he was able, John would leave a message with an old family friend in Europe. His parents were to wait ten weeks before Emily would call to ask if the package had arrived. A yes would signal a successful escape. A no would be his epitaph.

John had to assume that customs would be watching both the airport and the train station, which were constantly monitored by video cameras perched overhead. Canada and Mexico were both colonies of the United States when it came to intelligence matters, so there was no possible escape over land. And John knew that whatever the Feds missed, Murray's friends in the Mob and the IRA might pick up.

It soon became clear why it would take ten long weeks before John could communicate with his parents. John dragged a life raft and two survival suits out of the cellar. He was waiting until dark to make his escape by sea, breaking all the rules, just as his father had done. His father assumed that he had arranged to be picked up by a freighter leaving Boston Harbor for South America—a sea journey of ten weeks. November wasn't the safest time to take to sea in a rubber raft, but that made a sea escape a more unlikely and therefore more attractive option. A lifetime's romance with the sea—from his youthful adventures in his red dinghy to the *Valhalla*—had prepared John for this voyage.

John's father smiled bravely at his son. He crushed whatever doubt he had behind this smile. John would escape, he told himself, just as he and Emily had escaped from the communists. Heart disease and cancer would probably kill him before he could see John again, but someday he hoped that John would be able to return to the United States and live in peace.

"You ready?" he asked simply.

"Yeah," replied John dryly. "My ride will be here any minute. I've got to stop by the safe-deposit box first, I've got about five grand there. Then I'll cash my VA check. That's enough to get me started. Don't worry. I'll be fine."

Just before noon, John's pickup pulled into the driveway. Mr. McIntyre didn't want to know who was driving. John loaded his gear into the truck and took a seat on the passenger side. He turned out the window and waved good-bye.

9

THE PACKAGE
THAT NEVER ARRIVED

"Where's John?" Robbi demanded. "Where's John? Where's John? He was supposed to meet me at the Hollow Restaurant at five o'clock last night. We had a commitment." Without waiting for the McIntyres to reply, Robbi began her own search of their house, running from room to room and screaming "He had a commitment, that bastard, where is he?" over and over again as she went. John senior, Emily, and Chris were waiting for her when she returned to the living room.

"Now tell me," John senior said slowly, "what really went on last night?"

"He broke a most important commitment last night. He had a commitment and he didn't even show up," answered Robbi.

Robbi suddenly realized it was John's plan to double-cross both her and Brady at the Hollow Restaurant the night before. "Oh my God, oh my God," cried Robbi. "He set me up."

Mr. McIntyre gave her a cold, deliberate gaze. "You betrayed him to the police," he said bitterly.

Robbi turned and ran out the front door without replying.

For the next two days, she searched for a clue to John's whereabouts. On Monday, she discovered his pickup in the parking lot of Murray's home-heating-oil business in Charlestown. Robbi knew of John's growing dread of retribution by Murray. She began to fear that Joe had kidnapped John and killed him.

Robbi returned to the McIntyres' home to tell them of her discovery—and her fears.

If John was dead, said John senior, then it was Robbi who had killed him. She was the one, he reminded her, who had originally betrayed him to the police.

Robbi sobbed out a denial, but the McIntyres had seen with their own eyes the unusual police detail dispatched to arrest John. McIntyre had also done his own investigating. The police logs, he told Robbi, proved that the cops were on their way to her apartment before John had even arrived. Robbi, he charged again, had made a deal to inform on her own boyfriend.

Between tears, Robbi attempted to defend herself. She would never betray John, she insisted. She had done only what was necessary to protect him.

John senior was repulsed by her excuses. He had heard the logic of treachery too often to soften his heart before Robbi's transparent rationalizations. He ordered her out of his house. He had no way of knowing, at the time, that Robbi was ultimately not responsible for what had happened.

After Robbi left, the McIntyres weighed the meaning of her news. There was no good reason for John's truck to be at Murray's. He was plainly the last person John wanted to see on the day of his escape.

"Robbi was probably making that up to see what we'd say," McIntyre suggested. But he knew that Robbi wasn't capable of such subtlety. Her evidence suggested that John had been intercepted before he could make his getaway. McIntyre wondered aloud whether he should have advised his son to escape earlier.

★   ★   ★

The Package That Never Arrived

On Tuesday, December 11, 1984, the nonjury Special Criminal Court in Dublin, convened specifically to hear national-security cases, convicted the crew of the *Marita Ann*. Sean Crawley, Provo leader Martin Ferris, and the *Marita Ann*'s captain, Michael Browne, each received ten-year prison terms for arms trafficking. In reporting the sentences, the Irish and British press lauded Washington's cooperation in the case.

On December 13, the *Valhalla* story broke in Boston. The *Boston Globe* article carried the explosive headline "Boston Informer's Tip Led to Seizure of IRA Arms Papers Say." Lifted from reports published a day earlier in the *Times* of London and the *Guardian*, the article carefully pointed to the existence of an unnamed informer in Boston as the source of the information exposing the arms transfer.

"According to similar stories in both the *Times* and the *Guardian*," noted the *Globe* report, "the tip was the result of an internal investigation by U.S. Customs agents into British complaints that IRA sympathizers within the agency were facilitating IRA arms smuggling. After the identification of several suspects, part of a 'customs-service Emerald Society,' an informer was cultivated who told the customs service that a large cache of weapons was being put together to smuggle across the Atlantic.

"Officials of the U.S. Customs Service would not comment on the reports yesterday, although knowledgeable officials said they had been told some time ago the U.S. authorities had not been the original source of the tip that led to the seizure of the Irish trawler, the *Marita Ann*. They suggested that the reports could be a result of the 'Irish government protecting its own sources . . . They would be happy to throw undeserved bouquets at us, and we'd probably be content to accept them.' "

Philip Brady's first thought when he read the *Globe* article was that if John was indeed being held by the IRA, the story would kill him. Beyond that, the article had all the telltale marks of officially inspired disinformation. The London dateline and the reference to pro-IRA moles in customs clearly suggested that British intelligence was the report's primary source. The false information about the extent of America's and particularly customs's, foreknowledge of the *Valhalla*'s departure was clearly an attempt to protect their own sources and methods. But like all good disinformation, the lies were misted with shades of truth. How, Brady wondered, did the British know about an American source, his source?

John's name was never mentioned in the article, but the McIntyres were heartsick when they picked up the *Globe* that morning. Murray would immediately conclude that John compromised the *Valhalla* and *Ramsland* operations—unless, of course, Murray himself was the informer. The article, Emily noted, said that customs knew about the *Valhalla* before it had even left port in September. Yet John had no contact with Brady until mid-October.

Emily read the article repeatedly that day. She decided that it was a transparent attempt by determined customs agents to get even with John. The article was more proof that the Feds were trying to blackmail him into seeking their protection and testifying against Joe Murray.

John senior had another explanation, but he didn't have the heart to tell Emily. The London dateline effectively discredited her theory identifying customs as the source of the disinformation. British intelligence, McIntyre concluded, must want to deceive the IRA about the real source of the leak on the *Valhalla* operation. John, it was clear, had been targeted as the Boston informer—but by the Americans, the British, or both? Was their purpose merely to force John to seek their protection, or did they know that he would not be able to deny their lies? Were Washington and London, he wondered, colluding in the deliberate framing of a man they knew was dead? John senior didn't dare ponder such questions. There were still eight weeks to wait for his "package" to arrive.

A few days later, the McIntyres were presented with another piece of chilling news. John's blue pickup, the same one Robbi had spotted at Murray's, was found parked under the Neponset Bridge in Quincy.

Charles Allen was an expert in spotting abandoned vehicles. Allen, a tow-truck operator, was paid a bonus by his boss for each one he hauled in. He wouldn't ordinarily have bothered with a truck parked in the private lot under the bridge, but he couldn't help noticing that the blue pickup had been sitting for days with its windows down. If it had been July, Allen's curiosity wouldn't have been piqued. But it was December, so he went over to take a look.

On the dash, Allen found an envelope with the McIntyres' Squantum address. He phoned a friend on the Boston police force and asked him to trace the truck's license plates.

The owner's address matched the one on the envelope. Allen asked if he could be authorized to tow the truck to his garage. His friend did him a favor and approved, even though Quincy was outside his jurisdiction.

Allen called the McIntyres to tell them the truck had been towed. Mr. McIntyre told him to bring the vehicle over immediately.

"Found this on the dashboard," Allen said to McIntyre, handing him the envelope. "Thought it shouldn't get lost."

When John senior opened it, his ailing heart skipped a beat. Inside was John's VA check. If John hadn't cashed this check, thought McIntyre, he must be in real trouble. For the first time, he had some hard evidence to justify his brooding fears for his son's life.

John senior was hospitalized soon after the first of the year. The energy and spirit that for years had enabled him to defy his doctors' diagnoses of imminent death was now leaving him. Cancer and heart disease were finally winning their battle against time.

As the ten-week anniversary of John's departure approached, McIntyre's health improved enough so that he could be discharged from the hospital. He went home to Squantum, where, with all of his remaining strength, he waited for the telephone message that would put an end to his anguish.

Valentine's Day brought no news from Europe. Emily decided to phone her German friends herself, but they had nothing to report. John had left ten weeks before, promising to relay word of his safe escape. The silence on Saint Valentine's Day meant that their "package" had never arrived. The McIntyres had waited passively these long weeks, afraid of hurting John's chances for survival by initiating inquiries. Suspicious of both the U.S. government and Joe Murray, they now determined to undertake their own investigation to uncover the truth about John's disappearance. McIntyre had to know for certain whether John was dead and who was behind the disinformation campaign in the British and American presses. Discovery of one answer would, he was certain, lead him to the solution of the second mystery as well.

The next day, he went to the bank where John had kept a safe-deposit box since his teens. Using a key John had entrusted to him years before, he verified that John had emptied the box on November 30. As he was about to leave the teller's window, McIntyre called upon his repertoire of espionage tricks to divert the attention of the clerk while he palmed the form showing that John McIntyre had opened his box that day.

During his service in Germany, McIntyre had worked with many operatives who were now at the height of their careers. He counted a presidential contender and a former NATO commander among his contacts from the border-crossing days. There were many people in the intelligence community who would gladly do him a favor, and there were others who would have no choice but to help him. John knew too many embarrassing details about American collaboration with the Nazis for his old contacts to ignore his requests.

McIntyre began with the allegations from British sources in the *Times* article that American agencies had had advance information on the arms transfer.

Old friends peeked into security files. Old enemies reluctantly accessed computer databases. McIntyre's sources raided every top-secret computer facility in the country for a trace of a vessel named *Valhalla*. John would have marveled at his father's ability to penetrate the most protected intelligence vaults in the country. Had he been able, he would have chuckled at the irony that the very same back channels that so unnerved him might contain the clues to his disappearance.

A search of the COSMIC files showed that there had been no prior communication between NATO agencies about the impending IRA arms deal between the *Valhalla* and the *Marita Ann*.

If there had been satellite monitoring of the *Valhalla* from the time she left Gloucester, as the British papers reported, then CIA logs of the TK—TELINT Keyhole—system could verify the placement of agency satellites run by the U.S. Air Force National Reconnaissance Office in the appropriate orbit. The cameras aboard these satellites are so powerful that they can photograph an officer walking across the Kremlin and identify his rank by the insignia on his shoulder. A check of the PHOTINT (photographic intelligence) systems, however, showed that there had been no U.S. satellite surveillance of the *Valhalla* at any time during her voyage.

Penetration of the Special Intelligence vaults, the international electronic eavesdropping operation run by the U.S.

National Security Agency from bases around the world, turned up nothing. Searches of the NADDIS system of narcotics trafficking information; ATEX, Treasury's network linking ATF computers with state-police systems; and DICSI, the Defense Intelligence Central Security Index, which swaps files among the army, navy and air force's investigative services, were similarly unsuccessful.

There was little comfort for the McIntyres in their confirmation that no one in American intelligence knew anything about the *Valhalla* before she sailed. The findings of McIntyre's old-boy network merely confirmed their belief that the U.S. Customs Service, perhaps in cooperation with the British, had implemented a deliberate disinformation campaign aimed at their son, prompting his murder by the IRA.

Brady had discovered something the McIntyres' search had failed to reveal. One of his colleagues had heard DeFago and Chris Nelson discussing details of the critical October meeting with von Raab and told Brady what he had learned.

Brady immediately confronted DeFago and Nelson. He was furious. Not only had he been kept in the dark about an important meeting on a case in which he was one of the lead investigators, but the identity of his confidential source—one of the key figures in the investigations of Joe Murray's arms-smuggling and marijuana-importing operations—had been telegraphed by his agency to British intelligence. To leak such information and then withhold it from both the source and his handler, he claimed, was a breach of the most elementary standards of investigative intelligence work. Because of such amateurism, Brady believed, John McIntyre was most probably dead.

Both Nelson and DeFago, as well as their superiors, were desperate to prove that John was still alive, if only to absolve themselves of responsibility for compromising his safety. For months, however, customs had been unable to find any trace of John.

By March, customs had convinced itself that the McIntyres were withholding information about John's whereabouts. Brady, ever the company man, was willing to give his colleagues the opportunity to redeem themselves by proving it.

Brady and DeFago went to the McIntyres' home, made polite inquiries about John, and noted their concern for his well-being.

McIntyre was not about to let the men he suspected of forcing his son to flee home and country off that lightly. He accused them of being incompetent idiots who had jeopardized John's life with their unprofessional shadowing and transparent disinformation.

Brady sheepishly protested that he had no idea what McIntyre was talking about. John threw him and DeFago out of his house.

Brady went to Robbi and asked for her cooperation. Perhaps she could get to the McIntyres while their guard was down.

Soon Robbi too came to visit. Although Emily blamed her for John's troubles, she wanted to see what her game was.

She didn't have to wait long. They sat together in the living room, which was simply furnished with an old easy chair and couch and adorned with gifts John had made, a checkerboard and wooden model of an old three-masted schooner. Robbi worked herself into a fit of tears talking about John's disappearance. Black mascara streamed down her cheeks as Robbi begged Emily to tell her if John was still alive. She broke down sobbing and went to the bathroom to search for some tissues.

It seemed to Emily that her presentation was too theatrical, even for Robbi. She reached over and opened the purse

Robbi had left on the coffee table. A voice-activated tape recorder was nestled inside.

Emily wasn't surprised that Robbi was now working her own scam with customs. She always suspected Robbi would betray her own mother if the price was right.

When Robbi returned, Emily was ready to record her own message to Robbi's handlers. Methodically and without a trace of emotion, she listed the evidence that pointed to John having been murdered before he could escape: the uncashed VA check in his abandoned truck, the well-informed lies in the *Globe*, and his failure to contact them during these long weeks. In a quiet, composed voice, Emily said she knew Robbi and the U.S. Customs Service had helped the IRA murder her son.

Robbi cried crocodile tears, protesting her innocence and her friendship with the McIntyres. Emily showed her the door.

Emily's tape-recorded charges made for difficult listening at customs. She had given voice to the fears that customs was too proud, and afraid, to admit to itself.

DeFago, however, was unconvinced. He insisted that Emily's evident lack of emotion, particularly her failure to cry when discussing the evidence pointing to John's death, could only mean that she knew John was alive. He and Brady decided to pay her another visit when she was alone and without the support of her husband or son.

John senior had been admitted to the hospital yet again. Emily was riding an enervating emotional roller-coaster. Her son had vanished and was feared dead. And her husband's multiple illnesses required an exhausting series of never-ending consultations and tests, none of which pointed to a happy ending to his growing incapacitation.

Brady and DeFago were waiting for her one afternoon when she returned home from her daily visit to the hospital. Emily understood immediately from their brusque manner that this was to be no social call.

The Package That Never Arrived

Brady walked through the front door of the McIntyre house, right by Emily. He baldly informed her that he feared John was dead. Brady looked to DeFago for encouragement for what he was about to say.

He told Emily about the industrial car crushers located at the Polarizer Company, home to a big mountain of rusted scrap steel rising on the shore below the Mystic River Bridge in Charlestown. Irish gangsters had killed her son there, Brady said, in a car crusher, just like the autos that had been sent for scrap. By now, Brady said icily, John was part of a mile-long patch of pulverized metal hulks.

Brady's cruelty was deliberate. As he spoke, DeFago, now the amateur psychologist, watched Emily's reaction to Brady's gruesome description of her son's death. Emily was too fatigued to replay her self-possessed performance with Robbi. For the first time, a representative of the U.S. government itself was telling her that her son was dead. Emily couldn't stand to hear more. She told them to leave and began to cry.

Beside herself with grief, Emily left immediately on a macabre search of the Charlestown junkyard. She could get no closer to the mountain of metal than the chain-link fence that surrounded it. There she stood, her face pressed into the fence, probing for some identifiable remnant of her missing son.

Brady and DeFago caught Emily yet again one afternoon between work and her daily visits to the hospital. DeFago demanded John's passport. When she told him she didn't have it, he started once again where Brady had left off. DeFago described the gruesome methods the Mob used for interrogation. Didn't John ever explain what would happen to him if Murray discovered he was an informant?

Even Brady was disgusted by DeFago's abusive lies. He had given DeFago and the others every opportunity to prove their theory about the McIntyres. Now he had had enough. As

193

DeFago readied another assault, Brady stepped in and practically pushed his partner out the front door.

Customs, however, kept up the pressure, and their mental torture of Emily McIntyre didn't stop. One evening, after she had returned from the hospital, the phone rang. It was the Quincy police. Her son, the voice said, was in custody at the staton.

"My son *John?*" she exclaimed. But almost as quickly, Emily caught herself. Perhaps they had picked up Chris.

She asked the officer to describe the man they were holding. He gave her a perfect description of John. Emily couldn't contain her excitement as she headed out the door. The news was too good to be true.

She was right. Emily reflected upon what she had just heard and returned to the house. She placed a quick call to the police station. There had been no phone call, she learned, nor was John McIntyre in custody. Emily was crestfallen. When would they stop testing her knowledge of whether John was dead or alive?

John senior, between the bouts of medication that muddled his thoughts, became convinced by customs's escapades that either the U.S. government itself had no idea of John's fate or it was too smart to entrust such information to fools like Brady and DeFago.

McIntyre had one last hope for some hard facts: an old friend in British intelligence he hadn't spoken to in almost thirty years. John had once saved the man's life when they were both young recruits. Today, he was a senior British-intelligence official. He owed John a favor, and it was time to call it in.

The circulation in McIntyre's legs was now so bad that he couldn't walk far without assistance. He prevailed upon Emily to drive him into Boston so he could make contact with his British friend. McIntyre was very cautious when it came to even the most elementary intelligence operations. He risked his waning health that day in order to shield his source's identity from prying government eyes.

He directed Emily to a Boston parking garage, where he struggled out of the car.

"Where are you going?" asked Emily.

"The less you know the better," McIntyre replied. He ordered Emily to wait for him in the car, and he disappeared into the parking garage's elevator.

Emily waited for what seemed to be a long time before her husband returned and bundled himself into the car. His source had agreed to steal all the British-intelligence files on the *Valhalla*. They had arranged to speak again in thirty days.

The next day, McIntyre was admitted once again to the hospital. He was living for the phone call that would clear up the mystery of his son's fate. As the date for the planned rendezvous neared, the hospital agreed to release him for a brief stay at home, provided he rested. But McIntyre had no intention of dying in bed. When the appointed day arrived, Emily once again drove her husband into Boston. It was bitterly cold, made even more miserable by a driving, freezing rain. John told Emily to drop him off at the Park Street T station, just down the street from the gold-domed Massachusetts State House. Emily was to keep driving in a circle around Boston Common, stopping only when he reappeared.

On one of her passes, Emily spotted John, slumped against a light post across the street from where he had left her. She couldn't tell if there were tears streaming down his face or if it was just the rain. Emily got out of the car and led her stricken husband back to it.

"They killed him, Emily!" he whispered with his last reserves of strength. "The bastards murdered him!"

McIntyre was too tired, too devastated by what he had just learned, to speak another word during the half-hour drive back to Squantum. Emily helped John into the house, led him to the couch, and tried to get the blood circulating in his legs.

McIntyre then told Emily and Chris that his source had obtained British intelligence's complete file on the *Valhalla*. They showed that contrary to press reports in Ireland, three of the five men captured aboard the *Marita Ann* had been taken to a secret location for "aggressive interrogation." Two had broken and agreed to become informers.

More important, however, was the information in the files about John. The Irish and the British, McIntyre's source reported, had their own spy close to the highest councils of the IRA. This long-time informant, not John, was the source responsible for the seizure of the *Valhalla* and its arms. When the British were tipped off about John's work on the *Ramsland* bust, they saw an opportunity to provide cover for their IRA mole and to confuse IRA efforts to find and punish the real double agent in their midst.

British intelligence coordinated the disinformation about John's role on the *Valhalla* case in order to throw both the IRA and the incompetent Americans, who had demonstrated on countless occasions that they could not be trusted to maintain the confidence of secret information, off the scent of the real mole. John was cleverly exposed through well-placed leaks to the press.

The campaign of press disinformation could only begin, however, after a two-man hit team from the Secret Intelligence Service dispatched from Bermuda made certain that "they would finish the job": John would never be able to refute the British lies. As far as McIntyre's source could determine, the Feds had not yet realized that British intelligence had assassinated, on American soil, a confidential source of the U.S. government.

McIntyre had no doubt now that his son had been murdered—not by Joe Murray, the Mob, or the IRA but by the professional assassins of Washington's closest ally. He himself had worked with assassins from SIS, Britain's equivalent of the CIA, and he knew them to be ruthless killers who wouldn't quit until they had accomplished their mission.

Gaunt, his face sunken and ashen, hardly able to breathe, John McIntyre lost the will to live. A few days after his last contact with his British source, he was readmitted to the hospital.

A contemporary of McIntyre's appeared one afternoon without invitation in his hospital room. He carried the blue military-intelligence cap worn by members of John senior's intelligence club. McIntyre didn't recognize him, but he noticed the cap. He assumed this surprise guest must be a new club member coming to cheer him.

This was no courtesy visit. The mysterious caller didn't introduce himself. After a few obligatory pleasantries, he began a monologue about John. He praised the intelligence of this "clever lad" and spoke with admiration about the block-and-tackle system he had devised to ferry the arms from the *Valhalla* to the *Marita Ann*.

Knowledge of that system put this unknown gentleman in exclusive company indeed. McIntyre knew the Feds themselves were ignorant of the means by which the arms had been transferred from one boat to the other. They assumed that the two boats had been lashed together.

McIntyre fought off the drowsiness induced by the pain killers. His blunted sensibilities couldn't determine whether this stranger's accent was English or Irish. But it was vital that he keep a clear head about what he was being told.

The man drew closer to the bed. Over the hissing of McIntyre's oxygen mask, he warned, "Stick to the cover story that the IRA murdered John. Remember you have another son."

The courier dropped the cap on the bed and turned to leave. As he headed out the door, McIntyre tore off his mask and strained to pull himself into a sitting position. He managed to shout "Go fuck yourself" before collapsing onto the bed.

When Emily arrived, she found her husband asleep, with the blue cap beside him. How thoughtful for John's friends to have brought him a new cap, she thought. Had she looked closer, Emily would have noticed that the cap was far from new.

McIntyre considered the courier's threat against Chris very seriously, particularly after Chris suffered a broken leg when his motorcycle was run off the road by a hit-and-run driver within days of the courier's warning. In one of his lucid moments in the ICU, he told Emily and Chris to find Clayton Smith. When they asked why, he replied cryptically that the courier had said something that had made him curious. If he was right, they would be able to determine how the assassination team was directed to John.

Emily had an address and phone number for Clayton in Cherryfield, Maine, which John had once given to his father. She rang the number for Clayton Smith. This Clayton Smith, however, sounded much younger than the seventy-year-old man who had befriended her son.

Emily asked if he had ever worked at Walton's Pier.

"He's done it to me again!" replied the man angrily. "I have the same name as his and he keeps giving out my address as his. That old fox has caused me all sorts of grief." He slammed the phone down.

Emily called him back at once. She was desperately looking for this other Clayton Smith, she explained. Her son was missing, and only he knew what had happened.

The man did have something, a rural postal route where he thought the sought-after Clayton Smith had once lived.

Emily and Chris made the long drive to Cherryfield, Maine, a collection of small isolated homesteads straddling

The Package That Never Arrived

old Route 1. There was plenty of time during the six-hour drive to wonder why Clayton, whom John had considered such a good friend, had given him a phony address.

Their search took them to a ramshackle farmhouse set back in the woods, a small, single-story Cape whose faded green clapboards hadn't been painted in decades. Old motors and disassembled cars littered the overgrown lot. Chris recognized Clayton's car—a red Mercury Montego with a black vinyl roof and a couple of Marine Corps bumper stickers—parked among some junked cars in the side yard. In the car's glove compartment, Chris found a medical bill in Clayton's name.

The porch light was on, and the door was unlocked. When no one answered their knocks, the McIntyres let themselves in. The house was barren except for a couple of chairs and a mattress leaning against a living-room wall. The dusty wooden floors were bare, as were the walls. In a corner, Chris spotted a black rotary telephone and an ashtray overflowing with hundreds of cigarette butts. The phone was dead.

Chris looked into the refrigerator and opened the sole bottle of Pepsi he found inside. The soda was flat. Emily disassembled the electric coffee pot. A gray mold had settled on top of the coffee grounds. The kitchen cabinets were empty.

"This is a safe house," said Chris with conviction. It had all the telltale signs of the lemon factories his father used to talk about.

Emily agreed.

They continued their search in the cellar. Both noticed that it had a dirt floor that looked as though it had recently been dug up.

"I'm going to get a shovel," said Chris resolutely.

Chris went at his morbid business until he was satisfied that his brother was not buried there.

Emily and Chris had discovered all they could about the

house. But the purpose of their visit was to confront Clayton directly for information about John. On their way out, Emily told Chris to leave a note for him.

On the back of the envelope he had pulled from Clayton's car, Chris wrote, "John left a letter with me for you. Chris McIntyre." He placed it in Clayton's mailbox.

Chris and his mother drove home to wait for Clayton's call. He phoned some days later.

"I want to meet with you, Clayton," said Chris. "John said that I had to held-deliver this letter to you. He was very insistent."

Clayton silently considered his response. "Do you know what's in the letter?" he asked.

"No," Chris replied. "I don't pry into John's business."

Clayton agreed to see Chris, and a meeting at the Howard Johnson Restaurant in Saugus, just north of Boston, was set.

When Clayton walked into the restaurant with his daughter and son-in-law, Emily and Chris were already waiting at the counter. After Clayton sat down at a table, Chris walked over and explained that his parents were afraid that John had been killed, and they hoped that he could help them. "Emily wants the opportunity to talk with you," Chris said.

Clayton reluctantly agreed. Chris beckoned to his mother to come over and sit down.

Emily apologized for bringing him out under false pretenses, but, she told Clayton apologetically, there was no letter from John.

Clayton was angry, but Emily was too concerned with her own agenda to take any notice.

"We took the liberty of going through your house and digging up your cellar," she said bluntly. "We found two ashtrays full of Camel cigarettes, and you don't smoke." At first Clayton insisted that he was still living there, but Emily replied that only the arms of the chair next to the phone were free of dust.

The Package That Never Arrived

"I had to leave six months ago," Clayton replied evasively, his eyes fixed on his coffee as he spoke. Someone, he explained, had torched the trailer he had been using at Walton's a few months earlier. He had become so afraid that Murray or the Feds were looking for him that he had gone to stay with relatives in Vermont.

"Mr. Smith," said Emily, "please look at me. Somebody is using your house. Who is it?"

Clayton said nothing.

"What about the cigarettes?" she asked again. They were John's brand.

"I'm not a well man," Clayton replied. "John came to see me right before he left. He said he had to go home and bury a cat. He told me that Murray was after him and that he had to run, that he wanted to take off in a couple of days for Bermuda or South America. I haven't heard from him since. But I think your son's alive, Mrs. McIntyre. He's one tough, smart kid."

Emily was ready to believe Clayton. Perhaps he was too frightened to admit that he had helped her son escape from Murray. But when she enthusiastically related their conversation to her husband, he just shook his head sadly.

John Loftus, an attorney, was a former investigator in the Justice Department's Nazi-hunting Office of Special Investigations. He had gone public with his controversial discoveries of U.S. Nazi postwar intelligence collaboration; John senior had seen Loftus's report on "60 Minutes." He had called Loftus, and the two had subsequently become good friends.

Chris and Emily were with John senior when Loftus walked into McIntyre's hospital room. Both McIntyres were exhausted from the countless hours spent at John's bedside. Chris was still on crutches; the broken leg he had suffered when his motorcycle was forced off the road had yet to heal.

"McIntyre," Loftus said to his bedridden friend, "you look like hell."

McIntyre smiled and coughed out a laugh from behind his oxygen mask. He appreciated Loftus's frankness, but he was struggling now. He had stopped all medication. When he died, he wanted his mind to be clear.

That afternoon, McIntyre exacted a promise from Loftus to assist Emily and Chris in their efforts to uncover the circumstances of John's murder by MI6 and to expose the negligent complicity of the U.S. Customs Service. He told his wife and son to trust Loftus and to inform him of what they had already learned.

John McIntyre lived by an old-fashioned code of honor. He taught his children that America's ideals were worth fighting and dying for, whatever the personal cost. McIntyre lamented his country's violation of its commitment to John, and he suffered with the knowledge that the principles so dear to him and his son had been betrayed.

Before he died, McIntyre wanted to revenge their travail. He decided to unburden himself of secrets locked away for a generation. McIntyre asked Loftus to record his affidavit outlining the collaboration of American intelligence agencies with Nazi war criminals in postwar Europe.

"Please state your name for the record," began Loftus.

"John McIntyre, 40 Ocean Street, Squantum, Mass."

"During the year 1950, were you employed by the United States government?"

"Yes I was."

"In what capacity were you employed?"

"7821 Composite Group, which was a front for an intelligence-gathering operation, covert."

"The 7821 was known as the Gehlen organization, right?"

"It was known as the Gehlen operation, right."

"And that was General Reinhard Gehlen, the former [German] intelligence chief on the eastern front?"

The Package That Never Arrived

"Yes, that's General Reinhard Gehlen."

"And the 7821 . . . was that not an organization where the U.S. government employed former German intelligence officers?"

"Yes, it is."

"Were some of those German intelligence officers Nazis?"

"They were. They had to be."

"Were some of those German intelligence officers war criminals?"

"War criminals? Yes. Some of them were war criminals."

"Is it possible that the American officers in Pullach attached to the Gehlen organization did not know the background of these people as Nazis, Nazi collaborators, or war criminals?"

"No, hardly. Impossible."

"Did the Gehlen organization ever carry out any smuggling operations in moving Nazis across the border?"

"Yes, they were involved."

"They were smuggling people across the border?"

"Across the border and out of the country . . . [to Linz] Austria and then down to Trieste."

"At the time you transported people across the German border to Austria, was that legal transportation across the border or covert?"

"Covert."

"And from Linz were they airlifted to Trieste?"

"The only operation I went on was the flight. Austria to Trieste with no stops in between. I would guard them across the German border, and we picked up a plane this side of Linz, and we'd fly them . . . down to Trieste. At that time, he was picked up by other individuals, at which point I [broke off]."

"So you never covered them beyond Trieste?"

"No, not unless I got nosy."

McIntyre was coughing more heavily now. It was becoming too exhausting even to speak. He finished his testimony that day with an ironic observation about America's code of ethics towards its Nazi collaborators.

"If you gave your word that you would help these people in the future, it was up to you to help them. You didn't pull any deal you could. They gave me a price and they gave them [the U.S. government] what we wanted." He ended with a humorous comment about Gehlen's inability to keep his operations a secret.

"Let's stop," said Loftus. "I'll come back when you've rested. We can finish this tape then, and I'd like to get your exact words down on what the British files say about the *Valhalla* cover-up. We'll worry about it tomorrow. Get some rest."

John McIntyre, Sr., died the next day.

10

CLOSING THE ACCOUNT

By the time of McIntyre's death, customs's double cross of his son had become the prime topic of interservice gossip in the corridors of Boston's JFK complex. DEA and FBI agents chuckled that revealing John's identity was typical of an organization so well known for its ineptitude that even British intelligence had derisively labeled it "the gang that couldn't shoot straight."

Despite its bungling, customs was the darling of the media, which had swallowed whole the lie that a customs informer had had foreknowledge of the *Valhalla*'s sailing. As every one of its bureaucratic adversaries knew, customs agents didn't discover the ship until they literally tripped over it at Pier 7. Yet each time a piece of the arms-trafficking puzzle was leaked to the press, customs was singled out for praise.

Eventually, someone in the DEA decided that it was time to shame customs publicly for its grandstanding and to expose the true story of the *Marita Ann*'s capture—or at least as much as the DEA knew.

On May 15, 1985, a headline in the *Boston Globe* announced "Story Tying Boston Informer to IRA Arms Case is Called a Subterfuge: No Hub Tip in IRA Arms Case."

"The initial tip that enabled Irish authorities to foil the

largest Irish Republican Army gun-running operation in a decade last fall came from an informant in Ireland, not Boston, according to sources familiar with an ongoing federal grand jury investigation here."

The *Globe* article reported that "the Irish government falsely promoted the story of a Boston connection in order to conceal the identity of its informant as well as its close cooperation with the British government, which helped track the two vessels involved in the attempted smuggling scheme, one source said. The United States, far from warning the British authorities of the impending arms transfer, did not learn of the operation until after it had occurred, the source added.

"The seizure of the *Marita Ann* by the Irish authorities," continued the article, "has been hailed as a model of transatlantic cooperation in the war against the IRA. The Irish, in particular, have liberally praised U.S. authorities based in Boston for warning them that the *Valhalla* was on its way from Boston across the Atlantic.

"Irish and British press accounts said a U.S. satellite tracked the *Valhalla* on its way to Ireland. The reports also said U.S. officials had first learned of the plot from a Boston informant who had come forward in connection with an investigation of British charges that a pro-IRA cell within the U.S. Customs Service was allegedly facilitating arms shipments.

"But a source close to the ongoing federal investigation here flatly denied this, saying that the initial tip in the gun-running operation came from an Irish informant, who alerted Irish police that the *Marita Ann* was about to leave its home port to go out on a weapons run.

"The Irish police staked out the vessel and confirmed that it was leaving port, the source said. Because they had no high-altitude surveillance capabilities, the Irish then asked the British for help. The British, for whom stopping IRA guns is a high priority—especially after the bombing last fall of the Grand Hotel in Brighton where Prime Minister Margaret Thatcher was staying—sent up at least two Royal Air Force Nimrod spy planes to track the *Marita Ann,* according to the source.

"One of the British planes got a photograph of the *Valhalla* and U.S. Customs at the American embassy in London was alerted, the source said. But authorities failed to stop the boat, which arrived in Boston October 12 unmolested. It was not until October 16, four days later, that customs patrol officers spotted the vessel tied up at Pier 7 and seized it.

" 'A couple of customs agents who would have a hard time finding a pie in a bakery just happened to look over and find it tied up,' said the source.

" 'The Irish government threw us the credit because they wanted to protect their informant. They were also worried about giving the appearance that they were flunkies of the Brits or working closely with the British against Irish men and women. That could be a political problem for them.'

"The source said the transfer of weapons from the *Valhalla* to the *Marita Ann* was made in darkness amid turbulent seas. Crews first tried to lash the boats together, but the seas were so rough they had to abandon that tack as the boats slammed together, and investigators have been able to match chipped paint on both the *Marita Ann* and the *Valhalla,* the source said."

The McIntyres were gratified to see a public repudiation of the lies against John, but the information in the article brought them no closer to discovering the details of his murder.

The author of the *Globe* article would never reveal his sources, but Loftus hoped that the source could be enticed to come to the McIntyres.

On July 16, Loftus informed several local reporters working on the *Valhalla* story that the late John McIntyre, Sr., in tape-recorded testimony, had accused the IRA and Joe Murray of his son's murder. Loftus hoped that news of the tape recording would find its way from the reporter to the source.

The next day, Philip Brady arrived unannounced at Loftus's office.

Loftus played the cover story just as John senior had asked. Customs, he charged, had tried to blackmail John into informing on Joe Murray. And when he refused, its clumsy surveillance prompted the IRA to kill him.

"Look," said Loftus, "if you know John is dead or alive, you've got to tell me so I can let the family know. They have suffered enough."

Brady gathered his thoughts silently for a minute. For months, his superiors had deliberately withheld from him vital information about his confidential source. Against his better judgment, he'd joined DeFago's pointless harassment of Emily McIntyre. Brady decided that he owed something to her search for the truth.

For more than an hour, Brady unburdened himself to Loftus. He maintained that he had never shadowed or pressured John. There was no need to. Until the day he disappeared, Brady insisted, he believed John was being fully cooperative.

Brady, in fact, still assumed that John really had intended to continue as a confidential source on Murray's drug gang after the *Ramsland* bust. When he failed to arrive for their meeting at the Hollow, Brady, who had brought along a twenty-thousand-dollar payoff plus some additional front money for a drug buy on another operation, immediately suspected that the IRA had grabbed him. By July, he too had concluded that the IRA was responsible for John's death.

But, Brady continued, for months after John's disappearance he couldn't explain how the IRA could have discovered

John's cooperation with customs. He insisted that he had done absolutely nothing to jeopardize John's safety. He had no advance knowledge of the incident in Heller's Bar or the twenty-four-hour watch that had so rattled John. And, Brady added, he had been very suspicious about the praise that customs had received in the press the previous December for its intelligence on the *Valhalla* arms transfer. No one in customs had known anything at all about the *Valhalla* before it sailed, Brady said.

Brady then explained how he had subsequently learned from two colleagues about von Raab's meeting with Ambassador Price. He surmised that Price leaked the information gained at this meeting to British intelligence. He told Loftus that he thought it probable that the British, after hearing from the U.S. ambassador, leaked word to the IRA that the *Valhalla* informant was in Boston. The IRA, Brady hypothesized, must have then ordered Murray to get rid of John.

Brady swore to Loftus that his superiors had deliberately hidden the truth from him. He hadn't learned of Price's meeting with von Raab until long after John had vanished.

Brady assumed that top officials in Washington had been convinced by London to protect its valuable Irish source by falsely pinning the blame on the unnamed Boston informant. No one had told him the identity of the true informer, but he guessed that the DEA, through its own sources, must have uncovered information about the British mole in Ireland and leaked the story to the *Globe* in order to embarrass customs.

Brady then made his pitch. If McIntyre's tape recording corroborated any of the evidence he had gathered, it might force Crossen and the Justice Department to expose the truth.

Loftus admired Brady's courage. He was taking a great professional risk by revealing to him what he believed about Ambassador Price's discussions with the British and pursuing a story that his superiors wanted to forget.

Loftus told Brady there was no tape. McIntyre, he said,

had died without recording a statement. Brady's revelations had, however, confirmed key details already known to the McIntyres and opened a new avenue for Loftus to pursue. He warned Brady that he owed it to the McIntyres to confirm Brady's information with the Justice Department.

Assistant U.S. Attorney Crossen was not at all pleased to learn of Loftus's knowledge of customs's indiscretions. His investigation had already suffered because of interservice bickering and posturing before the media. The more sensational the revelations about the *Valhalla*, Crossen feared, the more difficult it would be for him to keep embarrassing news of customs's betrayal of its confidential source—with its ramifications far beyond this one investigation—out of the public eye.

"Was John really killed because he was a government source?" asked Loftus.

"Yeah," replied Crossen. "We offered him the Witness Protection Program because we were concerned for his safety, but he refused. Now everyone I've talked to is pretty certain that he's dead."

It seemed that no one in the federal government knew that John had been murdered by the British; everyone wrongly suspected Joe Murray. The McIntyres decided to forsake the bureaucrats, who were hopelessly ignorant of important aspects of the story, and confront the administration's political appointees, who were responsible for John's demise.

On July 22, Loftus sent a bare-fisted letter to Attorney General Edwin Meese outlining the U.S.–British agreement to set up John for IRA retribution.

"On behalf of the deceased and the surviving members of the family," stated Loftus after explaining what the McIntyres had learned, "I request an immediate investigation into the circumstances of John McIntyre's death. To say that gross improprieties were committed by officials in Washington and London appears to be an understatement. The reckless endangerment of an informant's life for the sake of publishing disinformation is more than a breach of security procedures, it is a crime. It is murder, not merely negligent homicide, when the government knowingly exposes an informant to the IRA without even warning him of the danger.

"It is my earnest hope," continued Loftus, "that both Agent Brady and the father were each misinformed and that there is some reasonable explanation other than the reckless sacrifice of the son's life by careless government officials."

The letter was a clever piece of disinformation of its own. Loftus persisted in John senior's cover story that the IRA had killed John but offered the Justice Department the opportunity to redeem itself—to offer "some reasonable explanation"—and reveal details of the British-directed assassination to the family.

If the Justice Department failed to respond within thirty days, Loftus threatened to go public with his charges. He promised to file a civil action against the United States for John's wrongful death and to appear before Crossen's federal grand jury in Boston.

The Justice Department, confounding the McIntyres' expectations, stonewalled. In a letter responding to his request, Loftus was advised to tell what he knew to Crossen. But Crossen never called Loftus before the grand jury. As the months of silence dragged on, it became clear that the Justice Department wanted nothing in the court's record about any U.S. role in John McIntyre's death. Although they acknowledged to the grand jury in secret that John was the confidential informant they had code-named USC 1, the government continued to tell the public that John McIntyre, Jr., was simply a fugitive from justice. It wasn't until late 1987 that the U.S. Army placed memorials to Emily McIntyre's husband and son in the Cape Cod veterans' cemetery.

* * *

On April 15, 1986, Crossen's grand jury returned indictments against Joe Murray, Pat Nee, Bob Anderson, Sean Crawley, and John McIntyre for conspiracy and illegal arms trafficking.

The next day, agents from customs and ATF arrested Murray and searched his home in Charlestown. In his basement, they discovered photos of the *Valhalla* and a stack of newspaper clippings relating to the seizure of the *Marita Ann*. Agents also found eighteen weapons, five of which had been stolen. The remainder had been purchased legally by Joe and his wife Sue, both before and after the *Valhalla* operation. Three guns—two Fabrique National .32-caliber pistols and a Smith and Wesson .38-caliber police special—were of the type used by the British and Northern Irish police forces. There were also belts of .50-caliber ammunition and wooden boxes containing ten thousand rounds of 7.62mm ammunition, identical to boxes found aboard the *Marita Ann*. Various countersurveillance devices and radio-scanner systems were inventoried, as well as over one hundred pounds of silver bars. Joe, it appeared, may have been readying another arms shipment.

For the McIntyres, John's inclusion in the Justice Department's indictment was a declaration of war. Emily was outraged at Crossen's cynical effort to indict a man who had lost his life because of his decision to assist customs in its pursuit of Joe Murray.

She called a press conference for April 16, in which she and Chris outlined the agreement between Washington and London to target John in order to protect the British mole in the IRA.

"The two governments painted a bull's-eye on John McIntyre's back and didn't even tell him," announced Loftus to the press. "It was only a matter of time before the IRA killed him," he charged, continuing the fiction of IRA complicity. Ambassador Price's spokesman admitted that a conference

Closing the Account

about a Boston source had occurred, but denied revealing any identities to the British.

For the first time, the McIntyres had gone public with their campaign to discover the true circumstances of John's death. The target of their press conference was not so much the Justice Department, who they knew would not help, or the public, which would be indignant at the government's treatment of John, but the IRA itself. By declaring that the IRA had murdered John, the McIntyres, still fearful for Chris's safety, hoped to force the IRA to come to them with whatever information they possessed.

The strategy worked. A few days later, an IRA courier appeared unannounced at Loftus's office. "Murray didn't kill John McIntyre," he said to Loftus. "The IRA knows that he wasn't a traitor. They know who the real traitor was."

This is it, thought Loftus. He finally had an authoritative IRA source. He anxiously invited the messenger into his private study.

The emissary calmly explained how the IRA had suspected immediately after the *Marita Ann*'s capture that the operation had been compromised by an informer within its own ranks. Because John McIntyre himself had insisted on such tight security, the IRA quickly narrowed its search to a few suspects. Within days of the arms-smuggling fiasco, it found him—a high-level official with access to the top strategy meetings of the IRA and the Army Council of the Provos.

Through this mole, the British had discovered that the Provos had turned to small-time mobster Joe Murray, first for funds and then for guns. Every time Joe traveled to Ireland, he unwittingly gave British intelligence a progress report on his expanding operation at Walton's Pier. When John traveled with Joe to Amsterdam, a photographer from British intelligence was waiting.

"British intelligence doesn't know this, but their double

213

agent was court-martialed and executed by the IRA in early October 1984," the courier announced.

The McIntyres had long suspected that British intelligence would never risk the IRA interrogating John once London had decided to set him up as the *Valhalla*'s informer. They could not take the chance that he might convince the Provos of his innocence. So the British arranged for John to be murdered and then planted the story of the Boston informer, which they knew John could not deny.

But their efforts had been wasted. John had been killed to protect an Irish informant who was already dead.

"I am not sure if I believe you," said Loftus. "Before Mr. McIntyre died, a friend in British intelligence told him that two SIS agents came to Boston that day to make sure that John died."

"We have positively traced two British soldiers from the Special Air Service unit stationed in Lisburn, Northern Ireland," replied the courier. "They traveled to the United States via Toronto and arrived in Boston on November 30, 1984, wearing civilian clothes."

"What the hell are you talking about?" asked Loftus skeptically. "McIntyre's information was that they were SIS, not SAS."

The messenger explained that the two Secret Intelligence Service agents from Bermuda were only the trackers. The hit team was composed of two professional killers from the Special Air Service. It was standard procedure for an SIS team to trail the target and set up the hit and for the SAS men to do the actual killing.

But the British somehow knew to grab John on the very day that he had decided to skip away. Someone in Boston had to have tipped the British off.

"Who betrayed John to the British?" asked Loftus.

"What do you know about Clayton Smith?" replied the courier.

Closing the Account

Loftus said that Clayton had put to rest any doubts the McIntyres had about him after their visit to his home in Maine. He told the courier that he had been instructed by the McIntyres to protect Clayton. He had been a good friend to John and they did not want to involve him in any way.

"Did you know that Clayton Smith isn't Catholic?" asked the courier. "He isn't even Irish. He was born a British subject in Northern Ireland and once worked in a sensitive area of the Harland and Wolf shipyards in Belfast. Do you know what that means?"

The Belfast yards repaired British warships, he explained, which meant that British intelligence had to have vetted Clayton before he could be employed there. When Joe Murray led British intelligence to Walton's Pier, a computer search for an operative in New England to infiltrate his smuggling operation turned up Clayton Smith.

Unable to convince Murray to take him on as a crew member, Clayton was watching the *Valhalla* during the summer of 1984 when the Provo mole notified British intelligence that the arms shipment was imminent. Clayton called the McIntyres' home often enough to be certain that the *Valhalla* had left for Ireland and then had notified London of its departure.

John once again became a subject of interest when Ambassador Price revealed the existence of customs's confidential source. When Clayton, after meeting with John and advising him about freighters heading to South America, tipped off the British to John's plans, they had ample time to fly in both the SIS team from Bermuda and the SAS assassins from Ireland.

"The McIntyre family will never believe it," was all that a stunned Loftus could say. Clayton had betrayed John?

It was all in the transcript of Clayton's secret testimony before the grand jury, continued the messenger. In return for his testimony implicating John and Joe Murray in drug importing and gunrunning, Clayton had been placed in a protective program where no one could trace him.

But the Feds had yet to realize that Clayton was working for the British, explained the messenger, and that Clayton provided the information that ultimately led to John's murder. They still didn't understand that the British had assassinated an American citizen to protect two British spies—one in Ireland, the other in Boston.

"And what about John?" asked Loftus. "How do the Provos feel about him?"

"He is still a hero to the IRA," answered the courier. "All of the men on the *Valhalla* operation are heroes."

The IRA, he continued, had even mounted a rescue operation to free Sean Crawley and Martin Ferris from prison. Sean had used a smuggled cache of plastic explosives to blow out every door on their escape path but one. The last huge steel door only buckled, leaving Ferris and Crawley with no option but to surrender to the prison guards.

Only Sean, thought Loftus, could have identified to the British the owner of the blue military intelligence cap that mysteriously found its way to McIntyre's deathbed. If Sean was one of the two aboard the *Marita Ann* who had been turned by the British, it would explain why a trained demolitions expert like him just happened to run out of explosives at the most critical stage of the prison escape.

"What do the Provos think of Joe Murray?" Loftus wanted to know.

"I won't deny that Murray is an embarrassment," replied the courier uncomfortably, "but the IRA won't disown him. The Army Council blames itself for looking the other way when they knew how Joe was raising money for the cause. But Joe won't do too badly. The U.S. government has been ordered by the judge to turn over all of its files to Murray's defense counsel. They don't want to do that; too embarrassing all around. Joe will get a plea bargain and be out in a few years."

Closing the Account

*   *   *

On May 21, 1987, Joe Murray, Pat Nee, and Bob Anderson pleaded guilty before U.S. District Court Judge Joseph L. Tauro to four counts of violating U.S. arms-export laws. Murray had earlier pleaded guilty to drug charges stemming from the *Ramsland* sting and to income-tax infractions. As part of his plea bargain with Crossen's office, Joe agreed to turn over $563,000 in drug profits, in addition to assets seized under the federal racketeering statutes. It was peanuts. The IRS investigators concluded that Murray had made more than a million dollars in a single year.

Murray wore a conservative gray suit and wire-rimmed glasses at his sentencing hearing on July 1. He stood erect before the judge, hands clasped at his waist, speaking only to answer questions, offering no statement in defense of his actions. This was his first time in the dock, and he was more nervous than either Nee or Anderson.

"As far as I'm concerned," declared Tauro, "the drug case is the most serious. That's the national-security case to me."

Tauro sentenced Joe to ten years for the *Ramsland* affair and an additional five for the Valhalla gunrunning. Murray, who had also been given a two-year term for tax evasion, could expect to be paroled after serving about six years. Anderson and Nee would be free in less than three years.

The SAS agents who murdered John McIntyre will never be judged in a court of law. They were acting upon official government orders, firsthand knowledge of which still remains a closely held secret in the files of MI6. And the doctrine of sovereign immunity prohibits a private citizen from suing a foreign government. Only in the court of public opinion can the actions of the British government be judged.

The Customs Service tried to spread the lie that John had absconded with government funds, but when pressed by reporters for documents, threw a "National Security" blanket over John's files.

Assistant U.S. Attorney Crossen was asked about John at a press conference after Joe Murray's sentencing.

"Mr. McIntyre," he said soberly and without a trace of irony, "stands as a fugitive. There is a warrant out for his arrest. If anyone knows where he is, we'd be happy to pick him up and prosecute him."

APPENDIX

UNITED STATES DEPARTMENT OF JUSTICE
Office of the U.S. Attorney
Boston, Massachusetts

United States of America

vs.

John Doe

Before the Grand Jury
Room 2
U.S. Post Office and Courthouse
Boston, Massachusetts

Wednesday, April 3, 1985
12:20 p.m.

COMPLAINT NO. ____

Appearances:
Gary C. Crossen, *Assistant U.S. Attorney*
Witness:
Clayton F. Smith
. . . .

Q. Was there ever an occasion at Heller's where Mr. Mc-

Intyre told you about being involved in the making of a lot of money by illegal smuggling?

A. Yes.

Q. And do you recall any specific occasion when you discussed that with him and had a response to him about that activity?

A. Yes, I remember it.

Q. Would you tell us, please, what you remember about that meeting?

A. Well, I think that was—I want to be very sure of what I say. We had had a considerable number of drinks and prior to this he had kind of in a kidding manner had asked me about getting interested in making a trip in this particular business.

Q. Which business was he talking about?

A. He was talking about smuggling.

Q. What was he talking about smuggling?

A. Smuggling marijuana.

. . . .

The Witness: I had had, I had had quite a lot of talk directed at me as to how much this particular man respected my abilities around ships and my long experience and this kind of thing. And I taught Mr. McIntyre many, many things on a legal basis, like marine engines and various riggings and I showed him how to splice a hawser and wire cable and all this thing and this gradually evolved, you know. And he was, he mentioned one time he was looking at me as a father figure and this blew my ego up a little bit and it made me feel good. I had a young man, a young clean-cut man, anybody's ever seen him will say that he is, he's neat, clean and very soft spoken, and I taught him a lot of things on a legal basis long before we ever got into this thing. In other words, he gained my confidence. Does that answer your question, sir?

APPENDIX

Juror: So in other words, you had a sort of, let's say, a close working relationship.

The Witness: I had a close working relationship. I got to admit I was attached to the young man, you know.

Juror: And did you ever refer him to somebody else that, you know, initially when he started talking about this who might be more willing to do what he wanted?

The Witness: I never mentioned any names. I did mention several times that maybe he should look for someone else, but I never mentioned any names because I didn't know any candidates.

Juror: You say the operation had succeeded. Was the [sic] there any indication on how this ship, a foreign ship going into our port, would have been unloaded?

The Witness: That was not my business. When the ship was tied up to the dock, I was told that my job was done when the ship was tied up to the dock.

Mr. Crossen: Anything further? Thank you, Mr. Smith. You're all set for today, thank you.

The Witness: Thank you, ladies and gentlemen.

APPENDIX

United States Department of Justice
Office of the United States Attorney
Boston, Massachusetts

United States of America

vs.

John Doe

Before the U.S. Grand Jury
Room 1307
U.S. Post Office & Courthouse
Boston, Massachusetts

Wednesday, March 5, 1986
11:45 a.m.

DOCKET NO. ____

Appearances:
Gary Crossen, Esq., *Assistant U.S. Attorney*
Witness:
Donald DeFago

· ·

Juror: Who owned the Ramsland when the marijuana was on it?

The Witness: Well, it was owned by a woman by the name of Janna Aschuytte, A-s-c-h-u-y-t-t-e. She was living in Britain at the time.

Juror: Did she leave Britain or make other stops on the way over?

The Witness: Well, it came here from the Canary Islands. It was purchased and outfitted in a series of moves. It was

222

purchased in Norway and then moved to [a] couple different locations to be outfitted.

Mr. Crossen: Again I would suggest probably the way to handle this, given that only three of the grand jurors haven't heard this testimony before, is to put the prior transcripts before those in the grand jury that haven't heard it. And to the extent that there remains some questions, we could answer those questions by direct evidence.

Juror: Agent DeFago, I have one question. You indicated before that a lot of the information for the answers you just gave us came from John McIntire [sic]. It is our understanding that John McIntire disappeared some time ago. Has he ever resurfaced?

The Witness: We have not been able to locate him.

Juror: Thank you.

Mr. Crossen: You are still working on that; is that correct?

The Witness: Yes.

Mr. Crossen: Constantly?

The Witness: Yes. We are constantly working looking for him.

Mr. Crossen: Anything further, ladies and gentlemen? Thank you, sir.

(Witness was excused.)

APPENDIX

United States Government
Memorandum
File: B003BL400018 SFC/nec

DATE: October 29, 1984

REPLY TO
ATTN OF: Steven F. Crogan, *Special Agent*
Through: GS/A James M. Rafferty

SUBJECT: F/V VALHALLA: Investigative Status Report

TO: Christopher M. Nelson
Area Special Agent in Charge

The following investigative status report consists of information developed by the writer subsequent to the October 16, 1984 seizure of the F/V VALHALLA at the Boston Fish Pier for its alleged illegal exportation of weaponry from the U.S. to Ireland without the benefit of a U.S. State Department Export License.

1. On September 24, 1984, Irish authorities were notified by an undisclosed source that a shipment of arms was going to be transferred to an unidentified fishing vessel off the western coast of Ireland.

2. On September 25, 1984, Irish authorities dispatched the Irish Navy Cutters Emer, Aishing and Diedre to the West Coast of Ireland for the purpose of intercepting such a shipment. The crew of the Irish Navy Cutters were complimented [sic] by members of the Garda, the Irish police.

3. On or about September 28, 1984, firearms and ammunition were transferred from the F/V VALHALLA to the F/V

Marita Ann approximately 120 miles southwest of Ireland in the Porcupine Bank fishing area.

4. On September 29, 1984, the Irish Navy Cutter, Emer located the F/V Marita Ann approximately 2.18 miles off the West Coast of Ireland's County Kerry near the Skellig Rocks area. Guardia Inspector Eric Ryan and three Irish Naval officers boarded the Marita Ann and discovered the weaponry that had been transferred from the F/V VALHALLA. Inspector Ryan placed the five crewmen under arrest for arms smuggling without incident. All members of the crew and the F/V Marita Ann were brought to the Irish Naval Base at Haulbowline.

5. On September 30, 1984, the five crew members from the F/V Marita Ann were taken before a Anti-Terrorist Special Criminal Court in Dublin. The five crew members have been identified as follows:

   A. Michael Brown, Age 42 (Captain)
   B. Gavin Mortimer, age 23
   C. John McCarthy, age 26
   D. Martin Ferris, age 34 (as alleged IRA Commander for S. W. Ireland)
   E. John Crawley, age 27 (AKA: Sean Crawley: AKA Michael J. Kineavy)

6. On October 3, 1984, the Assistant Customs Attache, London, advised the ASAC, Boston, MA that the F/V VALHALLA was the "mother ship" that illegally transferred the weaponry to the Irish F/V Marita Ann and, as such, would probably be returning to a Northeastern U.S. port of call. Investigation conducted by the ASAC, Boston determined that the F/V VALHALLA, previously known as the Kristen Lee, had been seized in 1981 by U.S. Customs Agents from its owner/Captain, Robert

W. Anderson, for swordfish smuggling and had been sold at a July, 1984 U.S. Marshalls [sic] auction to a Leland Schoen for approximately $240,000. Leland Shoen has registered the vessel under the name VAL-HALLA which is controlled by Shoen's newly incorporated Massachusetts company, Leeward Inc., 18 Argilla Road, Ipswich, MA. Shoen has described the F/V VAL-HALLA's main business as "fishing and related shipowning activities."

7. Based on the aforementioned information received from the Assistant Customs Attache, London, the ASAC, Boston, MA assigned S/A and CPO personnel to specific tasks in furtherance of locating the F/V VAL-HALLA upon its return to the United States.

8. On October 16, 1984 at approximately 12:10 p.m., two CPO's located the F/V VALHALLA at Pier 7, the Boston Fish Pier, and immediately notified the ASAC, Boston.

9. On October 16, 1984 at approximately 12:30 p.m. a group of S/A's arrived at Pier 7 for the purpose of searching the F/V VALHALLA and to interview any on-board crew members. Upon arriving dockside, S/A's observed two white males departing the subject vessel and proceeding in an opposite direction, away from the VALHALLA. S/A's approached the two white males, identified their office and requested that both subjects submit to interviews relative to their affiliation with the F/V VALHALLA as well as the whereabouts and activities of the VALHALLA for the past several months. It should be noted that both subject crew members initially denied any connection with the VALHALLA.

. . . .

APPENDIX

Traceable

A. 30 revolvers;
B. 21 semi-automatic rifles;
C. 15 semi-automatic pistols;
D. 6 bolt action rifles;
E. 5 pump action shotguns;
F. 4 submachine guns
G. 3 lever-action rifles;
H. 1 derringer
I. 1 double-barrel shotgun;

Non-Traceable

(The firearms are identified as not being traceable because their serial numbers have been drilled out or ground off by the suspects)

A. 66 semi-automatic rifles;
B. 4 submachine guns;
C. 4 revolvers;
D. 2 semi-automatic pistols.

Also seized from the Marita Ann was a large quantity of various calibers of ammunition. The official inventory of the seized weapons has not yet been received. It is interesting to note that the IRA suspects allegedly went to the trouble of chiseling out manufacturing information stamped on various crates of ammunition.

14. On October 25, 1984, S/A's from the ASAC/BO, NY, the Strategic Investigation Munitions Branch and the Assistant Customs Attache, London briefed Commissioner Von Raab and the U.S. Ambassador to Great Britain, Price, relative to the investigative status of the F/V VALHALLA/IRA investigation. Ambassador Price re-

APPENDIX

ceived a similar briefing from U.S. Justice Department Attorney and FBI personnel on October 26, 1984.

STEVEN F. CROGAN
[signed]

APPENDIX

United States District Court
District of Massachusetts

United States of America

Joseph P. Murray, Jr. and
Robert Andersen, Jr. [sic]

CRIMINAL NO. ____

Government's Statement of Facts in Support of Guilty Pleas to Information #2 (the Marijuana Offense) and Information #3 (the Tax Offense)

The government files this document to provide the Court with a comprehensive statement of facts to serve as a basis for a change of plea to Information #2 (the Marijuana Offense) and Information #3 (the Tax Offense) referenced in the Memorandum of Plea Agreement in Criminal No. 86-118-T. If this case were to be presented for trial, the government would introduce evidence as set out herein.

Statement of Evidence
Information No. 2

Throughout early 1984 (April–June), Clayton Smith, who would testify for the government, had a series of conversations with John McIntyre in which McIntyre encouraged Smith to participate in future marijuana offloads organized by Joseph Murray. Smith, whose testimony was referred to in the Statement of Evidence relative to Information #1, was working at the time renovating the vessel Surge and was being paid for this work by Joseph Murray. McIntyre told Smith that Murray was the man in charge of the marijuana import operations. After McIntyre made several efforts during this period to

229

convince him, Smith would testify that he eventually agreed to participate in the next marijuana load.

On a date in November, 1984 which witness Clayton Smith does not remember, Smith was awakened early and without prior warning by McIntyre. McIntyre asked Smith to help him dock a ship. They then drove to Quincy, MA, picked up some provisions and went to the Quincy Marina. McIntyre and Smith were joined at the Marina by Joseph Murray and Robert Andersen. Smith fixes the date of this event as several days before he was shown Boston Herald headlines by John McIntyre regarding the Coast Guard seizure of the Ramsland on November 14, 1984.

The four men had a meeting and were joined by one or two other men, who were not known by Smith. McIntyre and Murray outlined a plan at this meeting that called for a crew of men, not to include Murray, to rendezvous by boat with a large vessel ("over 200 feet long"), replace the crew of the large vessel and dock the ship with its cargo at the Army base in Boston Harbor.

Murray indicated that he would make sure there were people in place to assist in the docking and said in response to Smith's concern for the difficult weather prevailing that day that the weather was "not a factor in this operation." It was Smith's impression that Murray was in control of the meeting. Smith was also told by Murray regarding the ship, "if there's anything hot about her, it's in her keel."

After the meeting broke up, Smith, McIntyre, Andersen and the others boarded a white-colored sailboat ("Seven Winns") which had just arrived at the Marina, and which was owned and captained by William Winn.

The meeting at the Marina as outlined by Smith is corroborated by surveillance on November 14, 1984, which was being conducted at the same time by federal agents focusing on Joseph Murray, who observed Murray arrive at the Marina with Andersen and meet with a number of other people including John McIntyre, before the participants other than Murray boarded the Seven Winns.

The Seven Winns left the Harbor and Murray drove from the area, alone in his car. Smith has identified the crew members on the Seven Winns to be William Winn (the owner of the vessel), John McIntyre, Robert Andersen, Michael Nigro (currently a fugitive from Rhode Island) and another man, known to him only as John.

The Seven Winns proceeded out of the Boston Harbor and they then spent a long period of time with Andersen attempting to make radio contact with a ship. After a time, radio contact was made with the ship, and shortly thereafter Andersen announced that he and others on the bridge of the Seven Sinns [sic] had also sited a boat believed to belong to the Coast Guard. When the Coast Guard was sited, Andersen indicated that they would stay away from the ship they were intended to meet up with and head instead into Gloucester. The Seven Winns then proceeded into a pleasure boat marina, Brown's Boat Yard in Gloucester, arriving at about 2:00 a.m.

While the Seven Winns was at sea, the Task Force agents involved in this investigation boarded a Coast Guard Cutter, Cape Morgan, and began to conduct surveillance at sea looking for a large coastal freighter. After fixing on the vessel Ramsland by radar they followed it for several hours as it approached Boston Harbor at night in rough seas. While keeping an eye on the Ramsland, the Cape Morgan also noted by radar for several hours that a small white-colored pleasure craft was sitting outside Boston Harbor near a marker buoy. The commander of the Cape Morgan observed this pleasure boat at a distance with binoculars in the dark, as the Cape Morgan made a visual siting of the Ramsland. Shortly thereafter, at about 12:00 a.m., the pleasure craft headed north from the area. The time of departure of the pleasure craft noted by the Cape Morgan, the distance to Gloucester Harbor and the general speed which the Seven Winns is rated for are all consistent with a 2:00 a.m. arrival in Gloucester.

The crew of the Seven Winns, less Andersen, who lives in Gloucester, left the vessel and walked to a nearby doughnut shop. From the doughnut shop they arranged for two cabs and split up into two groups for cab rides back to the Quincy Marina and Somerville.

Two cab drivers, working that night for West End (Gloucester) Taxi, and the records of the cab company support Smith's testimony regarding time and place of pickup, destinations and number of passengers. The cab drivers did not recognize any photographs, but one cab driver indicated he dropped a passenger or two off in Somerville in a neighborhood within several blocks of Winn's home.

The Seven Winns remained in Brown's Boat Yard for two days, when it was moved by one Richard Geranian. Geranian would testify that he was called by William Winn and asked to move the boat from Gloucester back to its mooring at the Shipyard Quarter Marina in Charlestown. The berth at the Gloucester boat yard had been arranged the day before it docked there by a telephone call from Robert Andersen, who was known to the manager of the boatyard. John Fenton, manager of Shipyard Quarters Marina, where the Seven Winns is docked, indicated that William Winn had given him advance notice that the sailboat would be away from the marina for several days around this time.

While the Seven Winns was retreating to Gloucester, the Coast Guard was shadowing and eventually boarding the Ramsland with its crew of six British sailors, and its cargo of 36 tons of marijuana hidden in a fuel tank, running along the keel, beneath 200 tons of gravel.

A day or two after the seizure of the Ramsland, McIntyre stopped to visit Smith and showed him a Boston Herald headline regarding the seizure as noted above. McIntyre commented that it was fortunate that the Coast Guard moved when it did, rather than several hours later, because if they had waited they would have had a different crew (i.e. those from the Seven Winns including McIntyre and Smith) on board.

Information No. 3

The government would prove a substantial evasion of tax liability by Joseph P. Murray, Jr. during calendar year 1983, by proof of a substantial source of income from illegal activities (i.e., the marijuana import business) and vast expenditures of cash during that tax year.

With respect to Joseph Murray's illicit income the government would call as a witness Joseph Bangs, a former police officer and most recently a convicted felon. Bangs would testify that he and Arthur "Bucky" Barrett distributed large quantities of baled marijuana provided by Joseph Murray in 1981, 1982 and 1983. The focus of the tax prosecution would consist of the amount of cash transferred by Bangs and Barrett during 1983 to Murray and commensurate large expenditures during the same tax year.

Bangs' anticipated testimony is summarized below. Bangs and Arthur "Bucky" Barrett were 50/50 partners in the business of trafficking in marijuana. During the period 1981 through April, 1983, he and Barrett were together almost every day. Sometime early in 1981, Bangs was introduced to Joseph and Michael Murray by Barrett. The purpose of this introduction was that Bangs, being a partner of Barrett, could also do business with the Murrays. All the marijuana subsequently purchased from Joseph Murray was with Bangs and Barrett as partners.

Joseph Murray fronted loads of marijuana to Barrett and Bangs, acting as partners. After they distributed it and started collecting money, and within a few days, they would start to pay Murray off. Although Bangs and Barrett always split the proceeds evenly, Murray always looked to Barrett as the person responsible for payment for the load. The business of dealing with Murray for marijuana continued from 1981 until Barrett's arrest for conspiracy to distribute marijuana in connection with the seizure of 11 tons of marijuana out of a series of trucks and a warehouse in South Boston owned by Harbor Oil Company on April 6, 1983. Harbor Oil Company is controlled by Joseph Murray. Throughout the relationship the sale price by Murray for a pound of marijuana was at least $175 in 1981 and ranged up to at least $225 a pound in 1983, conservatively speaking.

Joseph Murray told Bangs that tractor-trailer loads went out to the Midwest before Bangs and Barrett got their loads, because Murray wanted to get rid of most of the marijuana before it started hitting the streets of Massachusetts. Shortly after it hit the street, locally, DEA would be out looking for the source of it.

Bangs and Barrett were generally contacted directly by Joseph Murray when a mother ship had been offloaded and Murray was getting ready to distribute it. A meeting place was arranged to work out the details of the transfer. The sales were always in truckload amounts ranging from 4,000 pounds to 10,000 pounds a load. All sales by Murray were fronted to Bangs and Barrett with Murray receiving his money shortly thereafter. The meeting places were generally at the Chelsea Produce Center, near the Commonwealth Pier, or near Murray's house in Charlestown. Bangs and Barrett would show up at the prearranged meeting place with a couple of trucks; they would give the keys to Murray who would then drive to an undisclosed location and load up the trucks. Most of the time Joseph Murray would pick up and deliver the fully loaded trucks to Bangs and Barrett. Bangs recalled one deal which involved two trucks. They stashed one at Howard Road in Medford and the other at Jake Rooney's daughter's house on Sylvester Road in Dorchester.

APPENDIX

Bangs and Barrett would take the fully loaded trucks to different locations, weigh and mark the bales, then reload the trucks. Bangs and Barrett had a digital scale. The weigh-ins would take place at the following locations: Howard Road, Medford; Sylvester Road, Dorchester; and Bangs' house in Tewksbury.

In January or February of 1983, Bangs and Barrett received their last big load from Joseph Murray. It was around the time that Marvin Hagler fought in Worcester. Bangs had tickets to go to the fight, but a big snowstorm prevented him from going. The load was received within a few days after the snowstorm. Bangs remembers Joseph Murray talking about how rough the seas were during the offload.

Murray was always paid promptly after the receipt of a load and was paid in full before Bangs got his share of the profits. Joseph Murray was paid no less than $2 million in 1982 by Bangs and Barrett. They also paid him $50,000 for some cocaine in 1982. Joseph Murray was paid no less than $1 million in 1983 for the 1983 load mentioned above by Bangs and Barrett. At that time the going rate for a pound of marijuana was around $225.

The system that Bangs and Barrett set up to get the money to Joseph Murray to pay for the fronted marijuana is as follows: Bangs and Barrett would start to pay Joseph Murray as soon as the money from their people started coming in. They would never pay any less than $100,000 per trip to Murray. There would always be $100,000 in each paper bag. At times Murray would be paid two or three bags at once. The $100,000 would be made up of $10, $20 and $100 bills. In the beginning Bangs would count out the money by hand; later on they acquired a money counting machine.

Most of the money drops for Joseph Murray were made in his house at Charlestown. Bangs and Barrett would go upstairs through Murray's living room and into the kitchen, off to the right and in the rear of the second floor. If Murray had visitors, he would ask them to leave or put them in another room. Murray would take the bag and put it into a kitchen cabinet above the stove or refrigerator, without counting it. This process would continue over the course of days until Murray was paid off for the fronted marijuana.

Bangs stated that he and Barrett figured that Murray was netting over $1 million on every load that he did with them and that Murray gave them a piece of the action on about 20 loads between 1981 and 1983.

Barrett and Bangs had a system of bundling the cash that they delivered to Joseph Murray. Each bundle would always have $5,000 in it. When $1,000 was put together, one elastic was put around the $1,000; then a $5,000 bundle would be put together with two elastics around the ends of the bills. The $100,000 bags were usually in the form of $50,000 in $100 bills and $50,000 in $20 bills.

Bangs further told us that Murray labeled every bale of marijuana with a number, starting each load with #101. Murray kept records so he would know who had taken what bales and who owed him.